T0129575

THE HE♥RT IN YOU

A Personal Journey through Your Physical, Emotional, Mental and Spiritual Heart

JEANNETTE M. NIENABER MEd.

BALBOA.
PRESS

A DIVISION OF HAY HOUSE

This book is a work of non-fiction. Unless otherwise noted, the author and the publisher make no explicit guarantees as to the accuracy of the information contained in this book and in some cases, names of people and places have been altered to protect their privacy.

Balboa Press books may be ordered through booksellers or by contacting:

Balboa Press
A Division of Hay House
1663 Liberty Drive
Bloomington, IN 47403
www.balboapress.com
1 (877) 407-4847

Because of the dynamic nature of the Internet, any web addresses or links contained in this book may have changed since publication and may no longer be valid. The views expressed in this work are solely those of the author and do not necessarily reflect the views of the publisher, and the publisher hereby disclaims any responsibility for them.

The author of this book does not dispense medical advice or prescribe the use of any technique as a form of treatment for physical, emotional, or medical problems without the advice of a physician, either directly or indirectly. The intent of the author is only to offer information of a general nature to help you in your quest for emotional and spiritual well-being. In the event you use any of the information in this book for yourself, which is your constitutional right, the author and the publisher assume no responsibility for your actions.

Any people depicted in stock imagery provided by Getty Images are models, and such images are being used for illustrative purposes only.
Certain stock imagery © Getty Images.

Print information available on the last page.

ISBN: 978-1-9822-2572-8 (sc)
ISBN: 978-1-9822-2574-2 (hc)
ISBN: 978-1-9822-2573-5 (e)

Library of Congress Control Number: 2019904200

Balboa Press rev. date: 04/24/2019

DEDICATION

For Ryan, Darren and Sean

ACKNOWLEDGEMENTS

With gratitude to all of my family, friends, teachers and
especially, my husband John for believing in me.

ILLUSTRATIONS AND TABLES

CONTENTS

PART 2: THE ENERGY OF YOUR HEART

PART 3: YOUR EMOTIONAL HEART

INTRODUCTION

"...basically there is only one major energy, life energy...and the heart center is where the principle of life is found."
—Alice Bailey.

Aristotle, once wrote, "The whole is greater than the sum of its parts" and it now seems this principle applies to all living things. Glimmers of its global significance surfaced in 1949 when Aldo Leopold wrote *A Sand County Almanac*. As the fledging science of environmentalism grew, it soon became apparent that all life—from microscopic algae to human beings--is best understood within the context of its **ecology**. Life shapes how organisms behave as much as organisms shape life. Together they co-create an amazing web of life.

Alice Bailey believed the heart carries the principle of life. If this is the case, then the web of life is struggling. According to the World Health Organization (WHO), the number of deaths on our planet from heart disease and stroke increased globally by 2.6 million people between the years 2000 and 2012. In 2012 alone, an estimated 17.4 million or 30% of the fatalities were due to these conditions. Alarmingly, this number is almost double--57%-- for those in the middle and upper-middle socioeconomic groups. Clearly, access to the best in modern health care does not guarantee a healthy heart nor is it not related to income.

Social media such as Facebook and Twitter were launched in 2004 and 2006 respectively. They are consistently branded as great networking tools to help us feel more connected to one another. Has the advent of social media really helped improve our quality of life? Are we really any more connected in ways that truly make a difference? The 2017 report by World Health Organization (WHO) is sobering. An estimated 322 million peoples suffer from depression. Not only that, from 2005 to 2015, in the same time frame as the explosion of social media, the number of reported cases of depression increased by 18.4 %. The statistics for anxiety are equally discouraging. There has been a 14.9% increase in depression since 2005, which translates into as many as 264 million humans living with anxiety. This too reflects a 14.9% increase since 2005. Humanity is currently experiencing unprecedented increases in heart disease, stroke, depression and anxiety to name a few. Without a doubt, the heart center is under siege.

Over the years, I have been fortunate enough to have travelled and lived amongst some of the wealthiest and some of the poorest people on our planet. As a child, I remember grumbling when my parents wouldn't buy me something I wanted and they frequently reminded me that, "money doesn't buy happiness". Years later, my children reacted in the same manner when I echoed my parents cliché. In 1980, while travelling in SE Asia, I became acutely aware of the separation between money and happiness. There, in remote mountain villages, I saw people working terraced rice paddies, living in simple houses, with no running water or electricity. Elsewhere, others lived and worked over the river in houses built on stilts. They played and bathed in this river regardless of the poisonous snakes and sewage. Despite the harshness of their physical existence they emanated laughter, joy and hospitality. The children had no school and wanted me to be their teacher. They inspired me to learn and understand as much as I could about the human heart and this book is its fruition.

As *The Heart In You* unfolds it reveals and integrates the physical, emotional, mental and spiritual aspects of the human heart. The flow of information and activities in this book is based on the latest scientific models and draws from many eclectic sources. The layout is designed in a progressive manner to create a self-care and self-aware toolbox filled with insights, and resources that can be used immediately. It is highly recommended the book be read in the sequence presented, as each part is fundamental to the next. For clarity, this book is divided into five parts, as follows:

1. **Part One** lays the foundation for connecting with and tuning into the heart. It begins by exploring *Your Physical Heart* from a personal perspective and includes an overview of the basics of this amazing organ. Highlights of how the heart responds in various circumstances are integrated with its anatomy and physiology in order to provide personal meaning for the reader.

2. **Part Two** unveils the dance between energy and the nature of matter. *The Energy of Your Heart* begins with the discovery of electricity and magnetism and flows into a discussion of the quantum atom and its implications for the human experience. This section is rounded out with a look at the ecology of subtle energies and the energy fields of the heart.

3. **Part Three** *Your Feeling Heart*, is designed to bring greater awareness of the important links between the chemistry of the body and emotional experiences. The activities and discussion assist with deep heart healing and guide the reader towards personal reflection, understanding and the wellbeing of their emotional heart.

4. **Part Four** builds upon the previous chapters as it addresses *Your Mindful Heart*. Here, contemporary ideas about the mind and heart are considered along with the basics of communication between the brain and heart. Topics such as biofeedback, meditation, and mindfulness are included in this part.

5. **Part Five** is the culmination of the earlier sections and integrates them into the wisdom of *Your Spiritual Heart*. The conscious and unconscious manner in which beliefs and choices energetically shape the relationships of the heart to that of self, others, and the cosmos are contemplated.

To get the greatest personal benefit from this book, engage in the activities, explore the ideas and use the opportunities provided for heart-centered reflection. Useful diagrams and video links accompany many of the topics. May *The Heart in You* be an amazing voyage and richly profound!

PART 1

YOU AND YOUR PHYSICAL HEART

"Transformation of the world begins with transformation of oneself at the level of one's heart".
—**Alex Grey**

Overview

Every year, thousands of students are taught that your physical heart is a mechanical pump designed to circulate the blood. Not only was that my own experience; I taught it from this perspective for 35 years. Obviously, this is not new information. In fact, I have a textbook, *Science for Today,* published during the 1930's that my grandfather used when he was a teacher. In a chapter called *The Human Machine* your heart is introduced as follows:

> *"The most important pump in the world. A little over three hundred years ago William Harvey, an Englishman, announced his discovery that blood circulates through the body and is kept moving by the heart. This announcement was received with laughter, and it was long before the facts of the circulation of blood were generally accepted."*

Today, the metaphor of the heart as a pump is considered general knowledge. However, as you think about this quote, you might wonder why it took over three hundred years for scientists to accept that blood is circulated by the heart? Will it also take another three hundred years for scientists to agree that the heart is more than just a "pump"? It is somewhat disheartening (excuse the pun) to note that the basic scientific concepts taught in schools have changed very little in over one hundred years.

Education it would seem, and humans in general, are very reluctant to revise their ideas of how things work. Research such as that of Driver and Erickson (1983) discovered that by the age of five, children have developed their own ideas about how the world works. These ideas, known as **naïve conceptions**, become ingrained and are very resistant to change. Moreover, unless challenged, these ideas stubbornly persist throughout adulthood. Consequently, the focus of Part 1 is not a simple anatomy lesson on your heart as a pump. It begins by inviting you to connect with your heart from a personal perspective. The goal is to understand and interact with your physical heart --from rest to stress— so you can move beyond your naïve conceptions and begin to work synergistically with your heart.

CHAPTER 1

YOUR RESTING HEART

1.1 Beginnings

"Beginningless beginning and endless ending"
—Buddhist saying

Three weeks after you were conceived, your body measured a mere 3 mm and, within its core, a tiny tube-like organ began to pulsate--the genesis of your heartbeat. By the fourth week this tube transformed into an amazing four-chambered organ that is your heart. As you developed, your embryonic heart grew in sync with you. All the while, each and every heartbeat ceaselessly nudged blood throughout your growing body, forging intimate connections with all aspects of your being.

The sound of your heartbeat can be heard six weeks after your conception, and it changes each time. Every beat sends information about the nature of your activities, thoughts and emotions. From the very beginning, to the present moment, streams of energy ride the subtle waves of your heartbeat sending messages in many different forms including: mechanical, biochemical, sound and electrical. Each type of energy carries its own rich cascade of data; which imprints the cells and tissues of your body with information, on many levels, long before you were born. This lifelong dance between you and your heart begins well before you have any significant brain activity and is so subtle, that these messages slide below your normal levels of awareness.

For all of these reasons and many more, your heartbeat is an important window into the ecology of your health and wellbeing. Beginning with the first activity, you will become familiar with your resting heartbeat and later on, how it changes under different circumstances. Try to approach these activities as if this was the very first time you have listened to your heart. Be a beginner as you listen to the dance of *The Heart in You.*

1.2 Getting Acquainted with Your Heart

> *"Zen mind, beginners mind, always be a beginner."*
> **—Shunryu Suzuki**

How well do you know your fantastic heart? In what ways do you affect your heart and vice versa? It's been my experience that we seldom ask ourselves these questions. More often than not, busy schedules make checking in with your heart a low priority. Yet, what could be more important than getting to know and understand this intimate organ? This section begins with a few basics about your physical heart and then, thru Activity #1, provides an opportunity to explore the **zen** of your resting heartbeat. Each activity is linked to the concepts presented in its section and includes reflective questions for your consideration. (It may help to color the diagrams included in the book if you wish.)

To begin with, your physical heart is composed of a unique type of muscle called **cardiac muscle**. It has a different structure and nature than the **skeletal** muscles used to consciously move your body. For example, cardiac muscle cells have specialized discs inserted (intercalated) at the end of each fiber to increase the efficiency and speed with which electrical signals are transmitted. Astonishingly, cardiac muscle cells are capable of beating on their own when isolated in a petri dish and, if fibers from different hearts are placed in the same dish, they will spontaneously begin beating with the same rhythm.

I first observed this phenomenon over forty years ago, and still find it incredible that such tiny pieces of tissue have the ability to not only recognize one another, but also synchronize their contractions without any outside direction. Such behavior speaks volumes about the subtle manner in which cells communicate even though much has yet to be understood. An example of this innate sense of timing occurs on a larger scale during public events when people begin clapping and then one rhythm becomes dominant and everyone starts clapping together in the same rhythm.

Left on its own, cardiac muscle beats 100 times per minute. In your body, however, the beat is regulated by a several systems that exchange signals with your heart. Blood circulating in your extremities i.e. arms, legs and skin, is one of these systems. Known as your **peripheral circulatory system (PCS)**, it plays an important role in the control of your resting heart rate. Other regulatory systems and factors such as fitness, age, weight and general health impact your heart rate as well and will be discussed later on. For the moment, let's begin by exploring your resting heart as outlined in Activity #1. You may be surprised at what you learn!

ACTIVITY #1

EXPLORING YOUR RESTING HEART

Time:_10 minutes

Objectives: This activity is designed to help you explore your physical heart when you are in different stages of rest. As you progress through this and other activities, you may want to note your observations and experiences in the space provided, or keep a journal to record your experiences. Fig. 1 appears at the end of this activity and provides some useful visuals to accompany this exercise and the follow-up discussion.

Step 1: Make yourself comfortable either sitting or laying down. You may want to turn off the TV or cell phone and put a "do not disturb" sign on your door.

Step 2: Begin with the intention that you will maintain a neutral and somewhat detached awareness throughout this exercise. Discard any current notions you have of yourself or your heart and just be curious.

Step 3: Begin with a long slow inhalation deep into your chest and belly. Feel your chest comfortably expanding in all directions. Repeat this three more times and count how many seconds, on average it takes to fill and then empty your lungs. Inhalations _____seconds. Exhalations _____ seconds

Step 4: Now slowly draw your attention to the center of your chest over your heart and scan this area. What do you notice? Does this area seem tense, or relaxed? Briefly describe your present relationship with your heart.

Step 5: In humans, the tissues and muscles forming the heart are partially folded over and twisted into an upward spiral that resembles a fist. Make your right hand into a fist with the thumb slightly curved and place your fist slightly left of the center of your chest. By placing your fist here, you have a close representation of your heart's location, size and shape. Weighing less than a pound (approximately 300 grams), your heart lies protected beneath your breastbone. Inhale deeply and bring your awareness to this area again. Note any feeling or thoughts that come to mind.

Step 6: Next, twist your fist slightly upward and to the left side of the heart in a clockwise spiral. This action models the spiral movement of blood as it circulates through your heart. The position and contractions of the 4 chambers cause blood to flow in a spiral. The natural curve of your thumb shows the route of a major blood vessel (**aortic arch**) and its branches as your heart sends blood out to your head and upper body. What do you sense about the spiral pulsations of your heart?

Step 7: Continue to breathe slowly and listen to your heartbeat for 2 minutes. Try to drop into its rhythm as it rolls through your body. What does it feel like to you? Does this rhythm remind you of any particular music or song?

Step 8: Mimic your resting rhythm by tapping or vocalizing. Is the rhythm smooth and regular or erratic? Does it feel weak or strong? What else do you sense? There is no right or wrong in this exercise, just observation.

Step 9: Place your index or middle finger on one side of your neck and find the pulse in your **carotid artery** or you may use the **radial artery** found on the inside of your wrist. Tune into the rhythm and count the number of beats your heart makes in 20 seconds. Record this here _____. Multiply this by 3 to find the number of beats per minute. _____. The number of beats per minute equals your resting heart rate. How many times does your resting heart beat in a hour? _____A day? _____.

If you have access to a stethoscope you might want to use it to listen more closely to the sounds of your beating heart. If you have a fitness watch you may want to compare its read-out to what you experienced.

Step 10: Take a few more breaths and slowly wiggle your fingers and toes to bring your awareness back to the room. How do you feel now compared to before this exercise? What was this experience like for you?

Reflective space for Activity #1:

Your resting heart rate (as measured in Activity #1) indicates how hard your heart is working. For example, 60 beats/minute means that your heart pumps about 83 mL (1/3 cup) of blood every second (5 liters of blood/minute). This is equivalent to an astonishing 7,200 L of blood per day! Although you may be physically resting, your heart is always doing significant work.

Incredibly, each beat of your heart is based on the information available in that specific instant. For example, your heart monitors any change in the volume of blood returning to your heart and uses this information to vary the rate and force of every contraction. As long as this volume is within a specific (**permissive**) range your peripheral circulatory system (PCS) is largely responsible for controlling your heartbeat. For most people this range is usually 13 to 15 liters/minute but it may reach as much as 20 liters/minute in elite athletes.

As you become more attuned to your heartbeat, its subtle changes in rhythm can help increase your awareness of how you are reacting to any given situation. It is interesting to note that heartbeats vary from person to person so much so that each of us has our own unique pattern. The nature of electricity will be introduced in Chapter 4 including the electrical patterns of your heartbeat-- as in an **electrocardiogram (ECG)**-- and its connections to your heart sounds. Sound recordings and animations of a beating heart are fascinating and can be explored at the following links:

http://www.easyauscultation.com/heart-sounds

The Pathway of Blood Flow Through the Heart Animated Tutorial. https://www.youtube.com/watch?v=BEWjOCVEN7M.

1.3 Your Heart's Basic Anatomy

"The goal of life is to make your heartbeat match the beat
of the universe, to match your nature with nature"
—Joseph Campbell

Now that you have tuned into your resting heart, it is useful to look at some of your experiences. The goal of this section is to provide a map of your heart's anatomy and circulation. Such knowledge is fundamental to developing conscious control of your heartbeat and blood pressure. Obviously this takes practice but the benefits of being able to "make your heartbeat match the beat of the universe" are immense and will be revealed.

During Activity #1, you may have noticed your heart's characteristic two-part rhythm. It sounds something like "lubb" then "dubb". This sequence of sounds occurs because your heart is a double pump and consists of two systems--right and left. Each system has two chambers, a smaller collecting chamber (atrium) and a larger pumping chamber (ventricle). The Box Diagram in **Fig. 1** provides a simplified map of the route travelled by the blood through your heart. The first sound ("lubb") of your heartbeat is produced by the simultaneous contraction of both upper chambers (**atria**) accompanied by the closing of their respective valves. The "dubb" sound follows a fraction of a second later with the contraction of the lower chambers (**ventricles**) and the closing of their valves.

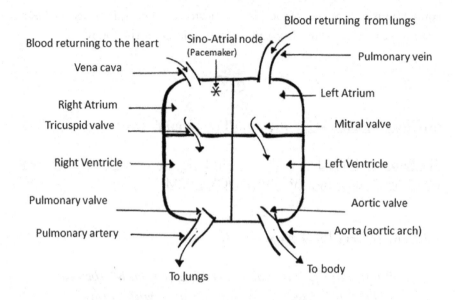

Blood returning from lungs

Blood returning to the heart

Sino-Atrial node (Pacemaker)

Pulmonary vein

Vena cava

Left Atrium

Right Atrium

Tricuspid valve

Mitral valve

Right Ventricle

Left Ventricle

Pulmonary valve

Aortic valve

Pulmonary artery

Aorta (aortic arch)

To lungs

To body

Fig. 1 Box Schematic of the Human Heart

The Box Diagram is a schematic map of the heart. The arrows on the map indicate the route of the blood. As it returns from the body, it enters the right atrium of the heart. It is then pumped through the heart to the lungs. Oxygen rich blood returns from the lungs to the left side of the heart and is pumped out to the body.

The choreography of these contractions is controlled by one of the most brilliant pieces of tissue in the human body. Often called the pacemaker, officially it is the **sino-atrial (SA) node.** Tucked away just inside the first chamber (**right atrium**) of your heart, the pacemaker is a highly specialized cluster of cells richly entangled with nerves. Its' unique nature is due to its ability to act as both a muscle and a nerve. When it contracts (like muscle tissue) it generates a nerve impulse (like nervous tissue) that travels rapidly throughout your heart muscles. This message reaches the upper chambers of your heart first and stimulates them to contract simultaneously making the characteristic "lubb" sound as blood is forced into the ventricles.

At the same time, this impulse travels to another node near the bottom of the right atrium called the **atrioventricular (AV) node**. Its job is to delay the impulses by 1/10th of a second to ensure the atria empty all the blood into the ventricles. The AV node tapers down into the **Bundle of HIS** which branches into the left and right ventricles. These fast-conducting, specialized fibers (**Purkinje fibers**) relay the signal and stimulate the ventricles to contract. Contraction of the ventricles and closing of the valves causes the "dubb" sound. Like the conductor in an orchestra the pacemaker creates the symphony of your heartbeat from moment to moment.

A good animation of the blood's circulation through the heart and lungs can be found on "Gas Exchange in the Lungs" at https://www.youtube.com/watch?v=AJpur6XUiq4

Fig. 2 illustrates the heart as it appears in your chest. As mentioned in Steps 5 and 6 of Activity #1, the chambers of your heart are folded and twisted into the shape of a fist although the pattern of blood flow remains the same as shown in **Fig. 1**. Contractions of the chambers twist the heart and cause the blood to flow in a spiral. A more detailed description of this sequence, beginning with blood returning from the body, is as follows:

1. Two large veins collect blood and deliver it into the first chamber of your heart (**right atrium**). One vein drains the upper body (**superior vena cava**) while the other drains the lower body (**inferior vena cava**).
2. As it fills with blood, the walls of the atrium stretch like a balloon filling with water. Specialized nerve cells (**baroreceptors**) embedded in the walls of the heart muscle monitor these pressure changes and send ongoing status reports to the pacemaker.
3. When stimulated by the pacemaker, the right atrium contracts and sends blood into the **right ventricle.**

4. Contraction of the right ventricle then sends blood out via the **pulmonary artery** to your lungs. This completes the right side of your heart's pumping system or the first cycle.

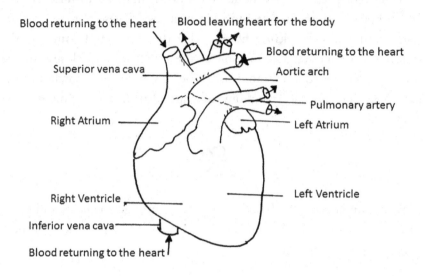

Blood returning to the heart   Blood leaving heart for the body

Blood returning to the heart

Superior vena cava

Aortic arch

Pulmonary artery

Right Atrium

Left Atrium

Right Ventricle

Left Ventricle

Inferior vena cava

Blood returning to the heart

Fig. 2 Basic Anatomy Diagram of the Heart

This diagram illustrates the shape and position of the heart as it appears in the chest cavity. Note how the spiral twist shifts the upper chambers or atria into the chest (dorsally) and towards the spine. At the same time, the left ventricle moves towards the front of the chest (ventrally).

5. As it approaches your lungs, the pulmonary artery branches repeatedly and eventually forms tiny networks of microscopic vessels called **capillary beds**. Nestled amongst your cells, these beds engulf the thousands of tiny air sacs (**alveoli**) present in your lungs.

6. **Carbon dioxide** and other wastes are released from the blood into the lungs. At the same time, **oxygen** is absorbed into the bloodstream from the air and binds to a carrier molecule in the red blood cells named **hemoglobin**. This process also changes the color of your blood from blue to red.

7. Oxygen rich blood then leaves the capillary beds, and gradually collects into a large vein (**pulmonary vein**) that returns blood to

the left side of your heart. Additionally, all entry and exit points for each of the four chambers are regulated via one-way valves to prevent backwashing of the blood when a chamber contracts.

8. The blood returning from your lungs re-enters your heart via the third chamber (**left atrium**). When this chamber contracts, blood is forced into the fourth chamber (**left ventricle**).

9. Having completed its second cycle, blood is propelled out of your heart into the **aorta** and **aortic arch**. All the major arteries branch out from this vessel and send oxygen rich blood to your entire body, including your heart!

10. Like high-pressure hoses, the major arteries have strong walls, thick with another type of muscle called **smooth muscle**. These muscles contact rhythmically to keep the blood pressurized as it spirals through the arteries and eventually reaches the capillary beds nestled amongst the cells and tissues of your body.

11. As blood passes through the capillary beds it collects wastes and begins its return to your heart where the cycle begins again-- endlessly replenishing and detoxifying all the cells of your body even when you are not thinking about it!

CHAPTER 2

YOUR DYNAMIC HEART

2.1 Linking Heartbeat Communication

"Volumes are now written and spoken about the effect of the mind upon the body. Much of it is true but I wish a little more was thought of the effects of the body on the mind".
—Florence Nightingale

Florence Nightingale wrote this quote well before scientists began to find evidence that the body, especially your heart, does in fact, affect your mind. Common phrases such as: heartache, heart's ease, bursting with joy, heart of stone and so on, describe strong feelings and thoughts associated with your heart. When you experience these "affairs of the heart" a cascade of biochemical messages and physiological changes ripple throughout your entire being. In this section, you will explore a few more of the systems controlling these changes. You will also look at how they impact you and experience some strategies—both ancient and modern--for working with these systems.

As you know, life is not just one long moment of rest. Increased movement increases, the amount of blood returning to your heart. At some point, it goes beyond the self-regulating or permissive range described in **1.2**. When this happens, the regulation of your pacemaker comes under the control of your **autonomic nervous system (ANS)**. The ANS acts as your body's information hub and works behind the scenes to control involuntary processes like breathing, circulation digestion, and elimination. Although vital to your existence, these systems generally function below your normal levels of awareness.

As shown in **Fig. 3**, your ANS consists of two systems that counteract one another namely:

1. **Sympathetic (SNS)** — Commonly called the *"fight or flight"* response. This system galvanizes your body for action. It's first of neurons (**pre-ganglionic**) originate in the thoracic and lumbar regions of the spinal cord
2. **Parasympathetic (PNS)** —The system promotes calmness and relaxation; which fosters healthy digestion and healing. Known as the craniosacral portion of the ANS, its pre-ganglionic fibers originate in the midbrain, medulla, and sacral portions of the spinal cord.

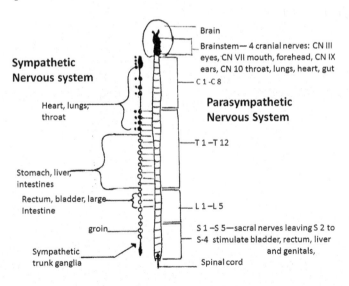

Fig. 3 Simplified Diagram of the Autonomic Nervous System and Spinal Cord

The brain, brainstem and spinal cord occupy the center of the diagram. The regions of the spinal cord are indicated to the right of the spinal cord i.e., cervical (C 1 – C-8), thoracic (T 1- T 12), lumbar (L 1- L-5), and sacral (S-1 –S 5). The stimulation of the parasympathetic system is indicated on the right side of the diagram and includes the cranial nerves (III, VII, IX and X) exiting the brainstem and the sacral regions (S-2 –S-4) of the spinal cord. The left side of the diagram represents the sympathetic nervous system; which connects to the sympathetic trunk ganglia via fibers leaving the thoracic and lumbar sections of the spinal cord. Both of these systems exist on each side of the spinal cord.

In Activity #1 you became acquainted with your resting heartbeat. The next activity draws attention and greater awareness to changes in your heartbeat. Recent research by Dunn et al (2010) demonstrated people tend to make better choices when they pay attention to changes in their heartbeat i.e. they listen to their heart! Moreover, this skill is especially important in challenging and/or difficult situations. Activity #2 is designed to help you explore your heartbeat under different circumstances so you can tune in with greater ease. The results will be interwoven with further discussion of the ANS and other important aspects of your physical heart throughout Part 1.

ACTIVITY #2

CONNECTING WITH CHANGES IN YOUR HEARTBEAT

Time: 15 min

This activity is about self- awareness and will increase your understanding of how you, your ANS and heart respond to a variety of situations. In Step 1 you will learn find the location of a few important ANS structures while in Step 2 you will listen to and record your heartbeat during four different scenarios. As Part 1 unfolds, the implications of each exercise will be discussed.

Objectives:

    A.   To locate and become familiar with the some of the centers related to your ANS.

    B.   Increase your awareness of some of the factors that cause changes in your heartbeat.

N.B. Please check with your doctor if you have any heart or health concerns before participating in this activity and adjust your activities accordingly.

Step 1: Use the following sequence to locate the following areas associated with your ANS. You may find **Fig. 4** helpful as well during this exercise

1. Slide the fingers of both your hands up the back of your neck on each side and feel for a ridge of bone where the base of your skull "sits" on the neck, this is called the **occipital** ridge. Many nerve tracts exit the skull just underneath this ridge.

2. Keeping your fingers on this ridge move them towards the center at the back of your neck. Gently feel for a small indentation. Here your spinal cord enters the skull and becomes your **brainstem.**

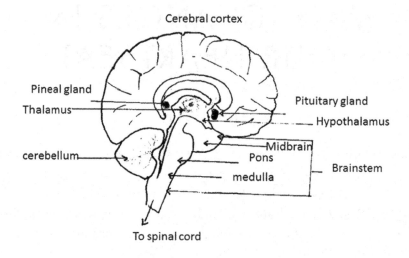

Cerebral cortex

Pineal gland

Thalamus

Pituitary gland

Hypothalamus

cerebellum

Midbrain

Pons

Brainstem

medulla

To spinal cord

Fig. 4 Basic Diagram of the Brain and Brainstem

The relationship between the brainstem and the surrounding structures of the brain are shown in this figure (sagittal section).

3. Next, using your fingertips, follow the curve of the occipital ridge outwards towards your ears and point them towards the opening of your ear canals. Imagine a line connecting your fingertips through your ears. At the midpoint of this line, you will find the lower portion of your brain stem called the **medulla oblongata.** It is here that your ANS processes and responds to incoming information.

4. Now imagine travelling up towards your brain. The brainstem bulges at this point to accommodate numerous tracts of nerves that link to your brain. This region is known as the **pons** and it is involved in communication amongst different regions of the brain, the regulation of breathing, sleep, and the senses, as well as, facial expressions.

5. Next, move your fingertips just in front of your ears and open and close your jaw until you locate the point where your jaw hinges. This spot is often tight when you are tense, and is called the **tempomandibular joint (TMJ)**. Note any tension or pain in this region.

6. Close your jaw and slide your fingertips down, in front of your ears to the hollow just under your jaw. This is where your Xth cranial or **vagus** nerve exits the skull. It is the longest and most complex of the cranial nerves. It interfaces with parasympathetic control of your ANS, and connects to heart, lungs, and digestive tract. It is considered a crucial information highway between mind and body hence it is often referred to as the pneumogastric nerve.

Step 2: Before starting, place your recording device or a journal nearby. Begin with about **one minute** of **rest** by sitting or lying comfortably and then take your resting heart rate as you did in Activity #1. Next complete the first exercise (**A**) for **two minutes,** take your heart rate, and rest for three minutes so your heart can adjust before you begin the next activity. You may use the rest period to record any thoughts, physical sensations, or emotions that arise during the exercise. Repeat the same protocol for exercises **B** and **C**. Throughout Activity #2 it is important not have any specific outcomes nor to dwell on any random thoughts etc., just be curious. (If you have a fitness watch you may use this as well for comparison).

N.B. if any of the exercises become uncomfortable simply note that you have omitted them and go onto the next one.

- **Exercise A:** <u>Moving You</u>. Walk quickly up and down the stairs, run on the spot, or perform any brisk physical movement that will get your heart and lungs working harder for 2 minutes. Take your heart rate and then rest (3 min.).

- **Exercise B:** <u>Breathing You.</u> Slowly inhale for 5 seconds, trying to expand the sides and lower part of your ribs to fill your lungs as deeply as possible, hold for 2 seconds and then slowly exhale for 5 seconds. Repeat this pattern for two minutes, take your heart rate, then rest 3 min.

- **Exercise C:** <u>Stressed You.</u> Remember a situation that is or was stressful for you. Observe as if from a distance or you are watching a movie. Don't try to change or engage in the situation. Notice how your heart and body react even when you are just imagining the event. Experience the stress 2 min., take your heart rate and then rest 3 min.

Observation Space for Activity # 2

Questions to consider:

1. Which of the exercises increased your heart rate and what if any, were the triggers?

2. Which of the exercises decreased your heart rate and what do you think might be the triggers?

3. Did you find any of these exercises useful for controlling your heart rate on a voluntary basis?

2.2 Moving you and your Heartbeat

*"Every human being should be able to perform
basic maintenance on themselves"*
—Kelly Starrett

One day, while at university, my chemistry professor marched into class with a stack of our papers and proceeded to berate us about our "black box" mentality. As he vented, we became increasingly nervous about our papers. Eventually we realized his anger was not directed towards us, instead it was about one of his PhD students. He had just failed his thesis defense despite impeccable work. Apparently, the problem arose when an examiner asked him to explain how his research equipment worked. His reply, "Well, it's just a black box" was not well received. Upon further questioning, they found he could not explain the basic principles behind the machines used during his research and therefore was not granted his PhD.

Over the years, I have been asked many questions about the human body. Some examples include:

- "Where is my stomach?"
- "I got diabetes and I don't know what it is!"
- "I've had two abortions and I still don't know how I got pregnant."
- "What is a stroke? I think I am having one!"
- "What and where is my prostrate?"

Questions such as these indicate that for many, their body is merely a "black box". If you use the metaphor of your body as a car, then your heart is its engine. It powers your body but if the tires are flat, or you run out of fuel, you aren't going very far. Each part of your car and/or body is important and works collaboratively with every other part to get you out and about. Sadly, most people take better care of their cars than their body and although I am not a mechanic, I can perform basic maintenance on my body.

The impact of the exercises in Activity #2 on your autonomic nervous system (ANS) will be discussed in upcoming sections to establish a basic understanding of how your heart, and autonomic nervous system exchange information to regulate your heartbeat. This information is incredibly valuable so that when your ANS goes rogue, you can learn to step in and restore balance before it gets out of control. Your body does not have to be a "black box" and you can learn to do maintenance on your ANS.

In Exercise A, of Activity #2, you were asked to move your body. Any movement of your skeletal muscles, even the thought of movement, stimulates the sympathetic side of the ANS to pump two very important chemicals into your blood stream:

1. **Epinephrine** (adrenalin) a hormone secreted by your **adrenal glands**.
2. **Norepinephrine** a neurotransmitter mostly produced by your **central nervous system (CNS)**.

The release of these chemicals has a powerful, global impact upon your entire body and automatically puts you on high alert. It is important to remember that this happens whether the threat is real or imagined--as in Exercise C. It is akin to revving the engine of your car and increasing its horsepower simultaneously –a rather amazing feat! That is not all these chemicals do, epinephrine and norepinephrine stimulate:

1. your heart to beat faster and increase the force of its contractions.
2. the smooth muscles lining your intestines and other internal organs to contract. This forces blood into your circulatory system and makes more blood available for your skeletal muscles should you need to fight or flee.
3. the smooth muscles in your arteries to contract causing an increase in both blood pressure and blood volume returning to your heart.

No wonder you feel ready to do battle! This surge of changes needs lots of energy too. Epinephrine also works to meet this need by stimulating the release of more blood sugar (**glucose**) and opening your airways to increase oxygen intake. The impact of epinephrine is so vast, that it is used as a therapeutic agent for emergencies and/or surgeries involving cardiac life support, allergic reactions, restricted airways and massive bleeding (**hemorrhage**).

Your SNS is essential to your survival. Unfortunately, nature did not intend for you to exist in a constant state of hyper vigilance. If left unrestrained, your SNS can run you into the ground and expressions such as "burnt out", "frazzled" or "exhausted" are apt descriptions of this state. Regardless of what turns on your SNS, long-term exposure to high levels of epinephrine and norepinephrine are hazardous to your health and side effects include:

1. high blood pressure (**hypertension**)
2. changes to the structure of your heart
3. damage to the arteries in your cardiac muscles
4. adrenal burnout.
5. autoimmune disorders such as Grave's disease, colitis, and cancer

For these reasons alone you need to pay attention to your heartbeat. Your answers to Question 3 in Activity #2 offer clues for slowing your SNS. More suggestions will be presented in the upcoming sections. Even though stress may be a fact of life, you can learn to recognize your triggers by listening to your heartbeat and developing successful strategies for calming your SNS. Everyone can learn to have a calm center or be the "eye of the hurricane".

Just as every warrior needs rest and relaxation after battle, so do you! Luckily, the other half of the ANS i.e. the parasympathetic nervous system (PNS) is designed to do to just that. It slows your heart rate and reduces the force of its contractions thru the release of a chemical called **acetylcholine**. Discovered in 1913 by Henry Dale, acetylcholine was the first substance found to transfer information between the nervous system and the body. Such chemicals are known as **neurotransmitters**. Until the ANS was understood however, acetylcholine was a bit of an enigma because although it slowed the heart, it also excites the skeletal muscles and stimulates movement.

Scientists were puzzled for quite some time as to how acetylcholine could have such different effects. As early as the late 1800's, it was suggested that different cells might have unique **receptors**—a bit like different passwords. Studies of the poison **curare**--known for its ability to immobilize skeletal muscle--held the answer. In the 1950's, using radioactive curare, P.G. Waser was able to photograph it binding to muscle cells in the gap where the nerves released acetylcholine. His work established the existence of acetylcholine receptors and showed that curáre paralyzed its victims by blocking the receptors in the muscle cells.

At the time, this was an incredible discovery and it was followed by a surge of research. Soon it became apparent that all cells have a huge variety of receptors. Like an array of antennae, receptors are embedded in the outer surface of every cell and each receptor binds only with specific messengers e.g. hormones, antigens, drugs, and neurotransmitters. When a receptor mates with its messenger, a cascade of changes is triggered. These changes vary with the type of cell and what it is designed to do. In the case of acetylcholine the receptors in your pacemaker and skeletal muscles differ and hence the same chemical can have opposing effects.

Evidently, your heart and the physical movement of your body are connected to both sides of your ANS. The relaxed (PNS dominant) state is linked to the release of acetylcholine and its ability to slow your heartbeat. While the alert, or SNS dominant state is excited by epinephrine and norepinephrine. Consequently, when you are more relaxed during an activity you can move with greater ease and less stress on your heart. Swimming is a good example. When someone is fearful of the water or doesn't like swimming their SNS is activated. This causes their muscles to contract and increases the tension in their bodies. It becomes harder to remain buoyant and often the individual becomes more panicked which makes the situation worse. On the other hand, someone who is relaxed in the water activates their PNS and can swim greater distances with less effort and a lower heart rate. Of course, other factors such as body density, stroke mechanics, fitness etc., affect the situation but this serves as one example of the complex interrelationships between exercise, stress, the ANS and your heart.

In this busy world, it is a constant challenge to keep your stress levels and SNS under control. The good news is you do not have to be a victim of your biology nor the roller coaster of life. It is possible to learn how to interact with your ANS and to maintain a life that has a healthy dose of the vegetative mode. Achieving this awareness is empowering and entirely possible if you are willing to engage in the process and find the tools that work best for you. In conjunction with these topics, the next section explores the currency of your energy and how exercise can help you and your heart.

2.3 Your Energy Bank

"Organic chemistry is the chemistry of carbon compounds. Biochemistry is the study of carbon compounds that crawl."
—**Mike Adams**

The popularity of leg warmers and funky headbands in the early 1980's was sparked by the release of Jane Fonda's **aerobic** exercise videos. I recall trying to workout with three small boys "helping mommy" by flopping on my stomach during sit-ups or trying to pull my leg warmers down as I ran in place. At that time, I was more inspired to lose my post-partum pounds than by the impact of aerobics on my heart. So what is aerobics and why does exercise have such an overwhelmingly positive effect upon your heart and health? To answer these questions, we first need to look at how your body stores and obtains fuel. In other words how do you put money into your energy bank? Here are some of the essentials.

Since the time of ancient Egypt yeast has been used to produce wine and beer. Traditionally a mysterious vital force found in living things, was believed necessary to create alcohol. This belief, known as **vitalism**, was shattered in 1897 by the Buchner family. They discovered how to change sugar into alcohol without using yeast or any other living source. Not only was the scientific world shocked, the Buchners' work sparked a surge of research into the chemistry of other biological processes. The field of biochemistry was born.

All life requires a constant supply of energy and as humans our social conversations often revolve around personal energy. Some common phrases include:

- "I just don't have the energy"
- "That takes too much energy"
- "I wish I had XX's energy"
- "I just can't get things done".

Such expressions often reflect fatigue, depression, or lack of motivation--topics that are also addressed in Parts 3 and 4. So how do living things obtain the energy they need to thrive? Food of course, supplies the raw fuel, but it must be converted into forms readily available to the body. Three pathways are elegantly designed to provide energy for your cells. They are illustrated in **Fig. 5** and consist of.

1. **phosphagen**
2. **anaerobic**
3. **aerobic**

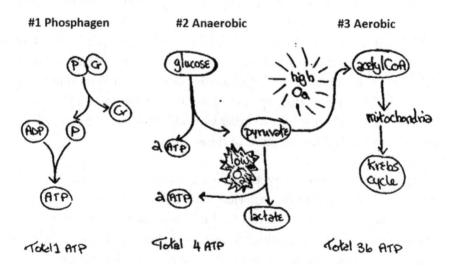

**Fig. 5 Three Energy Income Pathways:
Phosphagen, Anaerobic, and Aerobic**

Each pathway provides energy by producing an astonishing and unique molecule known as **adenosine tri-phosphate** or **ATP.** It is considered the energy currency of life. ATP is needed for:

- growth and repair
- building complex molecules
- contracting muscles
- generating electric currents and much more.

An estimated 1 x 10^{23} or one sextillion ATP molecules exist in your body. In any given instant, each cell contains enough ATP for 3 minutes of normal cell function—roughly an incredible one billion ATP molecules. In order to provide an optimal supply of energy, ATP must be formed, used, and regenerated in a rapid and efficient manner.

The main fuel for this amazing process is the simple sugar glucose. When the chemical bonds in glucose are broken, the energy is used to attach a third phosphate group (PO_4^{-3}) to **adenosine di-phosphate (ADP).** This creates a very special high-energy bond unique to ATP as shown in **Fig. 6.**

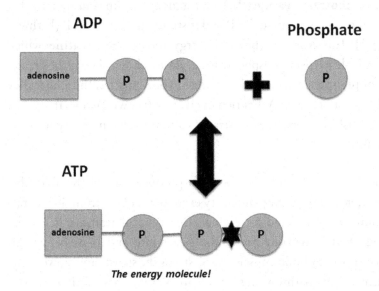

The energy molecule!

Fig. 6 Making your Energy Currency—the formation of ATP

When energy is needed, this bond is broken and the energy becomes available to the cell. At the same time, the loss of the phosphate group forms ADP; which becomes available to receive another phosphate group and rebuild an ATP molecule. This cycle is constantly repeating in healthy cells and each molecule of ATP formed is like putting money into an energy bank. No ATP? No growth, no movement, no thinking, no digestion, basically no life!

Just as maps have more than one route to a destination, cells choose from their options for making ATP. Each pathway has a distinct role and all are important for developing an efficient and robust metabolism. The greatest health benefits are obtained when all three are stimulated on a regular basis. This means your body needs a diversity of activities--yes, even with exercise variety is the spice of life!

When there is a high demand to move quickly, your body uses the phosphagen pathway. Typical movements involve short bursts of intense activity ranging from 10 to 30 seconds. Power lifting, sprinting, gymnastics and football are examples of such activities. The rapid production of ATP is produced by **phosphocreatine (Pcr)** a substance stored in your muscles. Pcr donates a phosphate group to ADP and instantly produces ATP (Pathway #1 in **Fig. 5**). This provides a burst of energy and releases **creatine;** which is then available to form phosphocreatine. Research has shown the greater the store of phosphocreatine and creatine in your muscles, the longer they can work without fatigue. A diet rich in creatine (i.e. wild game, free range meats, wild fish) has been demonstrated to improve your ability to move with intensity.

The second fastest way for your body to produce ATP is the anaerobic pathway. Short duration, high intensity exercise that lasts from 30 seconds to 2 minutes is considered anaerobic. This type of training is usually performed at 90% of your maximum heart rate and is used by non-endurance sports to build muscle mass, strength, speed, and power. The mechanism of this pathway was elusive for many years, until a team of biochemists led by Gustav Embden and Otto Meyerhof finally mapped the first part of the reaction in the 1940's. It was named **glycolysis,** which means *splitting of glucose*. This process occurs in the jellylike fluid or **cytosol** that fills and supports your cells. During glycolysis, one molecule of glucose yields 2 molecules of ATP plus 2 molecules of **pyruvate** (see Pathway #2 in **Fig. 5**)

The availability of oxygen determines which route is then used to obtain the energy remaining in pyruvate. If there is a lack of oxygen, i.e. you are "sucking air", the rest of the anaerobic pathway is used which ends in the formation of **lactate**. In a sense this is a dead end in the metabolism but it buys time as it shifts part of the metabolic burden from the muscles to the liver.

Additionally, This pathway leads to an acidic environment that causes muscle burn and nausea. I have vivid memories of being teased by classmates in high school for walking backwards up the stairs at the beginning of the Spring Training. The burning sensation in my legs was much worse than any humiliating comments I had to endure for my odd behavior. Today, many athletes help minimize the "burn" by immersion in cold water after a workout. This contracts the muscles and helps flush out the toxins as well as improve both cardio-vascular and lymphatic circulation.

The transition from pyruvate to lactate adds 2 more ATP molecules resulting in a total of 4 ATP molecules--3 more than the phosphagen route. The anaerobic route is shown as Pathway #2 in **Fig. 5**. It is interesting to note that the section from pyruvate to lactate resembles the conversion of pyruvate to alcohol by yeast. Hence, both are examples of fermentation, which reveals an underlying unity amongst the biochemistry of life.

Distance running, cycling, walking etc., are good examples of aerobic exercise. If you can still carry on a conversation while exercising, you are considered to be working aerobically. This means there is enough oxygen for pyruvate to enter the third or aerobic pathway. It is like winning the lottery in energy currency because during aerobic activity, pyruvate is converted into a substance that is transported into the powerhouse of the cell—the **mitochondria**. This substance is called **acetyl coenzyme A** and it enters a very special aerobic pathway called the **Krebs cycle** through which where the remaining energy is released (Pathway #3 in **Fig. 5**). The income stream from aerobic respiration is so rich that one molecule of glucose puts 36 ATPs in the energy bank. This is like earning $36 on an investment of $1!

This following You Tube video provides an amusing and helpful overview of ATP and its production called *ATP and Respiration: Crash Course in Biology #7—You Tube*

https://www.youtube.com/watch?v=00jbG_cfGuQ

So where do the Jane Fonda and other aerobics videos fit into all of this? In the 1960's, Kenneth Cooper a US Air force doctor was perplexed as to why some people with excellent muscular strength were still prone to poor performance at endurance tasks such as running, cycling, swimming and walking. Such tasks reflect a person's ability to use oxygen and are a reflection of their cardio-vascular fitness. The more efficiently the body can supply oxygen to the muscles plus the ability of these muscles to use the available oxygen the greater your cardio-vascular fitness. Additionally, your heart rate increases directly with the need for oxygen therefore, measuring your heart rate not only indicates the rate of oxygen consumption but also the type of metabolic pathway you are currently using. Maintaining a steady elevated heart rate at 70 to 75% of your maximum is considered aerobic exercise. Monitoring your heart rate, as in Activity #2, therefore provides a window into the type of metabolic pathway being used during any given activity.

Dr. Cooper's research was based on thousands of enlisted personnel, and eventually led to the 12-minute and 1.5 mile, fitness tests. His popular 1968 book *The New Aerobics* has undergone numerous reprints and provides an overview of aerobic exercise. More recently, Whelton et al reported in the April 2002 issue of the *Annals of Internal Medicine*, that aerobic exercise reduces blood pressure in individuals with both high and normal readings. The study recommended aerobic exercise as an important lifestyle component for:

- prevention and treatment of high blood pressure.
- increasing metabolism and hemoglobin levels
- increasing venous return and stroke volume of the heart
- improving the health of capillary beds
- increasing pH buffers in the bloodstream
- increasing chemicals such as endorphins that enhance your sense of wellbeing.

When you can experience such powerful cumulative and global effects, why wouldn't you want to exercise?

A useful chart relating activity level, age, heart rate and type of training at the following website:

https://commons.wikimedia.org/wiki/File:Exercise_zones_Fox_and_Haskell.svg#/media/File:Exercise_zones_Fox_and_Haskell.svg

(Remember these are general guidelines and it is important to get your doctor's approval before starting any new program and listen to what your heart is telling you.)

You may want to glimpse the symphony inside you every instant of your life. The following link to the biochemical pathways map provides an in-depth look at these complex processes.

http://biochemical-pathways.com/#/map/1 and

http://biochemical-pathways.com/#/map/2.

CHAPTER 3

BREATH, STRESS, AND YOUR HEART

3.1 Breathing Basics

"... conscious cultivation of breath offers a powerful way not only to extract energies from the outside world but also to regulate the energetic pathways of our inner world..."
—Dennis Lewis

Recall from *Beginnings* (**1.1**) that your embryonic heart began four weeks after conception. At the same time, some of the cells folded in towards the developing chest cavity. Once inside, these cells continued to grow into thick, tough fibers and formed the **central tendon.** Like a pillar of scaffolding, this tendon anchors your heart in the center of your chest and limits it's the vertical movement to less than an inch. Simultaneously, muscle tissue arose from the interior surfaces of the developing ribs to form the **diaphragm**. It grew towards the central tendon and became securely attached to this structure. Your diaphragm and heart thus share the same center, and since well before your birth, have never been apart. This relationship is shown in **Fig. 7.**

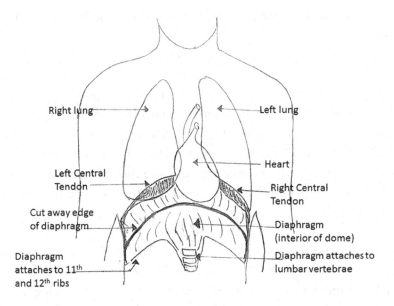

**Fig.7 Diagram of the Heart, Lungs and Diaphragm
indicating their relationships to one another and
to the Right and Left Central Tendons**

From your first breath to your last, the lungs and respiratory system are elegantly designed to bring air, specifically oxygen, into your body and release waste and toxins such as carbon dioxide. How often do you actually think about your lungs during your day-to-day activities? It has been my experience that most people are unaware of their breath until they physically exert themselves, or have a respiratory issue. There are volumes I could share with you about the magic of your lungs but for the time being, the breath exercises of Activity #2 and how they relate to your heart and ANS will be the focus.

How did you feel after **Exercise B** in Activity #2? Long, slow, deep inhalations are known induce a calming or relaxing effect. This type of breathing expands the tiny passageways or **bronchioles** that control the volume of air entering your alveoli. As they expand, they stimulate your PNS to release acetylcholine that in turn lowers your heart rate and induces a more relaxed or *vegetative state*; which is fundamental to a healthy life.

You can live with a deactivated SNS but without the PNS you will not survive.

In contrast, if your breathing is fast and shallow, your SNS is stimulated and begins to dominant and counteract your PNS. Rapid, shallow breaths are examples of the SNS in overdrive and often precede or aggravate anxiety, hysteria and panic attacks. When you or someone nearby is experiencing such an agitated state you can help them by staying calm yourself. Take some slow deep breaths and help them do the same. Holding their feet may help. Obviously if it is out of control you should get medical help immediately.

As a child, I had always loved swimming underwater because in those few magical moments between breaths, all was right with the world. In fact, I loved it so much that scuba diving and synchronized swimming became passions of mine. I had no idea about Yoga or breath work (**Pranayama**) at the time, but I knew I liked the calmness breath control gave me. The focus of Activity # 3 is to explore some of the connections between breath and heart rate control.

ACTIVITY #3

EXPLORING
YOUR LUNGS

Time: 10 min

Objectives: Your diaphragm is made of skeletal muscle and fibrous tissue. When relaxed, it forms an elastic dome shaped boundary that curves upward into your chest cavity and separates your heart and lungs from your abdominal cavity. This exercise is to landmark the anatomy of your lungs and to increase awareness of the interactions between your lungs, breath and heartbeat. This activity is best done lying down but can be done while sitting. You may refer to **Fig.7** while doing this activity.

Procedure:

1. Begin by taking your heart rate and record it.
2. Using your fingers, trace a line from the bottom of your chin, down under your jawbone and past the bulge of your voice box (**larynx**) to the V-shaped notch where your collarbones meet. This is called the **suprasternal notch** and it marks the uppermost (superior) section of your breastbone or **sternum.**
3. From the notch, continue down the center of your chest until you reach a small rigid protrusion, just past your last pair of ribs, this is your **xyphoid** process. Place your fingertips from both hands on your xyphoid and sweep them out and away from the center on each side in arcs that flow down and around the edges of your

lower ribs. Continue around your back to the point where your floating ribs attach to the top of your lumbar spine. The outline you have just traced is a good set of landmarks for the lower perimeter of your diaphragm and its attachments.

4. Now place your fingertips just under your lower ribs and observe what happens to your ribs and belly as you slowly inhale to the count of five.

5. Then exhale to the count of five. You may want to repeat this several times as you tune into the synchronized movements of ribs, belly and diaphragm. Are there any areas that move more or less freely than others? Does your breath fill and lower your ribcage or does it stop higher up?

6. Move your fingertips to your collarbones and once again slowly inhale and exhale to a count of five while you focus on breathing into the upper part of your lungs. Repeat as needed until you feel an inner connection with your breath and the movements of your upper ribs and collarbones. Do you notice any differences in your breathing between this part of your body and the lower ribs? Record your observations.

7. Now practice inhaling and filling you entire lung cavity. Using a count of 10 begin by filling the chest from the bottom of your diaphragm to the very top of your collarbones. Then slowly try and reverse the process i.e. release the air in small increments from top to bottom to the count of 10. Repeat 2 to three more times and then take your heart rate again. Record your observations and experience in the space below,

8. You may want to experiment by increasing and decreasing the counts for inhalation and exhalation as well as the number of repetitions to find a combination that works best for you.

Reflective space for Activity #3:

The mechanical design of the muscles and bones in your chest and abdomen provide resistance and stability to your diaphragm. This in turn optimizes the exchange of air between your lungs and the atmosphere. The greater your body's ability to move air in and out of the lungs, the more oxygen can be transported to your cells. The importance of oxygen cannot be understated and its crucial role was outlined previously in the section on aerobic respiration. Headaches, depression and fatigue are frequently alleviated through deep breathing. There are many studies that describe dramatic improvements in overall health through practices such as Yoga, Qi Jong or Tai Chi because they develop coordinated patterns of movement between breath, heart and body.

Inhalation is an active process as the muscles work to increase the volume of your chest cavity. Your diaphragm contracts and is pulled down towards your abdominal cavity. The muscles between your ribs (**intercostals**) contract and move your ribs out and away from the center of your body in a wing like manner. Simultaneously, the muscles around your sternum and collarbones contract and pull these bones upwards. The overall coordination of these movements results in an increased space in your chest cavity. This lowers the internal air pressure so air flows from the atmosphere into your lungs to equalize the pressure differences. Incoming air is approximately 20% oxygen and 0.3% carbon dioxide.

Exhalation, on the other hand, is a passive process. All the muscles of the diaphragm, ribs and sternum relax and pull inward and away from the walls of your chest reducing the overall volume of your lungs. This raises the internal pressure in your lungs above that of the atmosphere and the air flows out to equalize the pressure. Outgoing air averages 16% oxygen and 4% carbon dioxide.

Based on this synopsis, breathing sounds like a pretty straightforward process. However, most people exchange a much smaller volume of air than what is potentially available. For example, the average male can hold 6 liters of air in his lungs, but the maximum amount actually exhaled is 4.8 liters. During normal, relaxed breathing, a mere 0.5 liters per breath is the usual volume exchanged--although this varies with age, gender, size and health. Other factors such as the number of hours sitting at a computer, obesity and lack of exercise act to fossilize poor breathing patterns so that over time the muscles of your diaphragm, ribs, sternum etc., become restricted and reduce your capacity for larger volume exchanges. When this occurs, it becomes increasingly difficult to increase the amount of air inhaled when your body needs more oxygen during movement and/or exercise which in turn decreases health and well-being.

The following animations provide good insights into the movement of your lungs during breathing The first web address is a simple animation of structural changes during respiration while the second is a more detailed description of the structures discussed earlier.

https://www.classzone.com/books/ml_science_share/vis_sim/hbm05_pg35_diaghragm/hbm05_pg35_diaghragm.swf

https://www.youtube.com/watch?v=dTsUyXXudvA

In resting adults, the average breath rate ranges from 10 to 20 breaths per minute. The chart in **Fig. 8** shows the inter-relationships amongst the rate and depth of your breath and ANS.

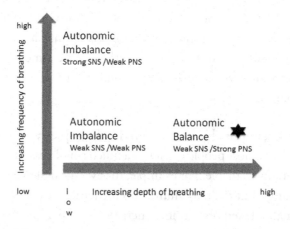

Fig. 8 Grid showing Relationships amongst Depth and Frequency of Breathing, to the Autonomic Nervous System

As you increase the breath rate but do not change the volume of air exchanged i.e. rapid shallow breaths, you stimulate the SNS and this in turn increases your heart rate as your body prepares for a fight or flight response. Slowing your respiration rate and taking deep breaths stimulates your PNS, slows the heart rate, and helps balance your ANS. Experienced divers and swimmers take advantage of this by pausing to take a few long deep breaths before swimming underwater. It not only lowers the carbon dioxide levels in their blood thus reducing the stimulus to breathe, but it also makes them more relaxed which reduces their rate of oxygen consumption. Both factors work together and enable them to stay underwater for a longer period of time.

In my private practice I frequently encounter clients with restricted and/ or elevated breathing rates. Often, as I begin a session, I ask the client to focus on taking a slow deep inhalation while they visualize breathing in beautiful clean air. Then, when ready, I have them exhale slowly with the intention of releasing or letting go of all that no longer serves. I ask them to repeat this cycle several times while completing my assessment. This stimulates their PNS and begins the process of relaxation that continues to deepen as their treatment progresses. More often than not, even in a safe, warm setting, the invitation to breathe deeply, results in a small increase in the movement of the client's upper chest.

As the session progresses and the client shifts into a deeper state of relaxation—snoring is often a good indication-- their inhalation usually moves to encompass the middle of their chest or **mid-thoracic** region. When I have finished a treatment, I have the client sit on the edge of my table while I do a "mini" back treatment that contributes, among other things, to a final balancing of the PNS and SNS. First, I gently use my thumbs and draw small opposing spirals on each side of the spine as I work up their back 3 or 4 times. This releases the muscles alongside the spine and stimulates the parallel chains of nerve ganglion that run beside the spinal cord. These chains of nerves are part of your autonomic nervous system. The thoracic and lumbar regions innervate your SNS while the sacral and brainstem sections activate your PNS (the location of these nerves and their connections to the ANS can be reviewed in **Fig. 3**).

Secondly, I place my hands over their lower ribs and adrenal glands and ask them to inhale slowly and push against my hands two or three times. Not only does this give the PNS another boost, it also helps calm the adrenal glands. Most people find this particularly soothing and it also gives me a chance to observe their most relaxed breathing patterns. I have found many clients have great difficulty breathing into the lower attachments of their diaphragm-- especially those who have unresolved stress and/or trauma-- and this is a subtle way to help them release ingrained patterns of tension. Breathing exercises may be assigned as part of their personal homework.

In the yogic practice of **Pranayama** (breath work), the goal is to free your body from restrictions of the breath. The root *prana*, means life or breath energy while *yama*, refers to restraint or control. Another interpretation is from the root *ayama*, which means to free the breath and hence honors both involuntary and voluntary control. Good breath work then is not so much about a rigid, upright posture it is more about releasing the muscular tension and habits that interfere with the body's natural wisdom. Many trained yoga instructors offer classes in this work. In the meanwhile, an easy way to improve both your lung capacity and posture at the same time is to imagine a cord pulling your breastbone to the ceiling when you inhale. This automatically adjusts the shoulder blades back and helps settle your head and neck into a natural and more comfortable position. As an added bonus, this alignment helps you look younger and feel more confident!

How does this all connect to your heart rate? Remember the central tendon described at the beginning of this section? This intimate connection enables the physical movement of your diaphragm and lungs to lightly massage the heart. Therefore, when you consciously bring your breath into a slow rhythmic pattern, you can do the same for your heart rate. Slow deep breaths not only stimulate your PNS, and restore balance to your ANS but, more importantly, they induce a slow steady rhythm in your heart rate. This synergy of the heart and lungs is a form of **coherence**. When the heart and lungs work together in such a manner it optimizes and amplifies their efficiency for moving blood and oxygen throughout your body, which serves to refresh and energize your entire physical body right down to the cellular level. The sense of calmness and well being that accompanies such coherence has many implications—some in ways we are only beginning to understand--others we will explore later on in this book.

3.2 Stressed you and your heartbeat

"...The deepest principles of yoga are based on a subtle and profound appreciation of how the human system is constructed. The subject of yoga is the self and the self is an attribute of a physical body."
—Leslie Kaminoff

When I was growing up, *stress* was not a common conversational topic and phrases such as "I am so stressed," "I have a really stressful job., or "this relationship is really stressing me out," were rarely used. Nowadays, it is unusual to enter into a social or work setting and not encounter these or similar phrases as a topic of discussion. Sometimes it even slides into a type of competitiveness as to who is dealing with the most stress or an analysis of why you are so stressed. The fact remains that stress has an obvious and immediate impact on your well being for both the immediate and long- term time frames. As a result, it is important to recognize what triggers your stress and develop your own personal arsenal for coping with your stress.

What is stressful for you may or may not be stressful for someone else. Tolerance levels for stress also vary from person to person and can be affected by numerous factors including health, age, lifestyle, and life experience. For example, if someone who is not afraid of spiders finds a large spider in their house, it is probably not a big deal, while someone who is allergic to them or seriously afraid could become very stressed even to the point of an anxiety attack. Often its not so much what the trigger is but how you react to it and the environment in which the event takes place. If you are afraid or taunted by others it can add factors such as humiliation that can amplify your stress in the moment and linger until the next time it happens. You might want to take a minute or so to jot down some of the situations you currently find stressful. Then some possible solutions that will enable you relax and decompress your reaction to these triggers.

My Stress is Triggered by: **Solutions to Help Me Relax:**

The list you have just formed is intended to help you establish a baseline so that you can learn to:

1. recognize what your body is telling you
2. learn to take conscious action
3. gain greater control over your reactions to stress.

You have already learned how exercise and breathing will stimulate your PNS and help calm you, so already you have two tools for restoring balance to your ANS. The more you are aware of issues that trigger the release of epinephrine in your body, the more you can consciously choose effective ways to compensate for and/or counteract its effects. Herein lies one of the most important gems of stress management.

Even though your ANS does not always require your conscious interaction, it is important to understand something about the nature of these internal signals and their control mechanisms. This will help you to interact with your body and its control systems in a more constructive manner. When you imagine your body as a machine on autopilot, as many of us do, it is easy to believe you are separate from your body. This separation leads you to disassociate even further from the natural dialogue between you and your body and can actually become a form of self-sabotage. Poor management of stress and ignoring signals such as high blood pressure, pain or anxiety drives you even further from the essential hub of communication between you and your heart. This creates a negative loop that feeds upon itself until one day you may find yourself at war with your own body.

Many years ago, a friend who had a very high stress job shared his strategy with me. He said, "Once I recognized that there was always going to be stress in my life, I realized I had to find effective ways to deal with it or it would win." Although it was very sound advice, at that time I was in survival mode and I couldn't even think about how to cope. I felt like I was running as fast and as hard as I could but no matter what I did, someone kept turning up the speed on the treadmill.

As a single mother with 3 small children, I was working full time as a science teacher and athletics coach and I used my lunch breaks to train for a ½ marathon. My parents, who lived 5 hours away, had serious health issues, I rarely got enough sleep and I was dealing with a chronic infection. It was a recipe for disaster so it was no surprise that one day I found myself observing my septic body lying in an emergency room while I floated above it waiting for death.

During those moments, my life started to pass before me, which was all pretty interesting until the birth of my children. At that instant, I realized I would not be able to raise them if I died now. It jolted me to another level of awareness that I have always remembered. I began to pray that I would live so I could raise my children. I also realized I was worth taking care of not just for my children but for myself too! Of course it was an extreme way in which to learn such a lesson and I sincerely hope that this book will help prevent you from such drastic measures. The personal insights regarding the *issues in my tissues* and why I needed to deal constructively with my stress were a gift in disguise.

That old saying "if the cup is empty no one can drink from it" has much meaning here. If you are always running on an overactive SNS, your ability to nurture others will be severely compromised. Unfortunately, I've had many clients who not only feel unworthy, but also tell me they do not know what it feels like to be relaxed or they simply can't relax. This lack of self-worth all too often goes along with nightmares and/or insomnia and far too frequently dovetails with deeper issues including abuse, trauma, and/or **Post Traumatic Stress Disorder (PTSD).**

Toddlers often find ways to self soothe such as thumb sucking, a favorite stuffed animal, or a blanket. Adults need to find things that bring them comfort too. Finding an activity that activates your PNS is a good place to start. Personally, I relish chocolate although there are many other ways to relax such as taking a hot bath, listening to music, creating something, gardening, meditating, receiving a massage, and so on. Remember that you are worthy of finding healthy ways to bring your ANS into balance. You do not have to do this by yourself either! Find a counselor or support group, seek medical advice, and engage in things you enjoy.

It is interesting to note that recent studies have linked the level of stress experienced by the mother during pregnancy to changes in fetal heart rate and neural development. What was experienced in the womb or as an infant often becomes the familiar comfort. So much so that those born into a stressed, tense home environment can feel uncomfortable, even stressed, when placed in a calm, relaxed environment. As the child matures this can set up an unconscious urge to create chaos and divisiveness in order to return to the perceived comfort zone of their childhood. Such situations can obviously perpetuate dysfunctional family dynamics such as bullying and abuse from one generation to the next. Herein lies the wisdom of making the effort and seeking support so that you can increase your personal awareness and begin shifting towards a balanced ANS.

Surprisingly, the position of your tongue provides a very quick and easy way to reduce stimulation of the SNS and balance the ANS. The **hypoglossal nerve** runs from the tongue to the back of the pharynx where the **brainstem** and **vagus** nerve can be easily accessed. The position of your tongue reflects the amount of tension you are undergoing and studies have shown by simply changing the position of your tongue you can voluntarily shift your ANS from alert to relaxed and vice versa. A relaxed tongue is soft and sits back towards the pharynx on the floor of your mouth with the tip just touching the back of your teeth. In contrast, a tense tongue pushes against the roof of your mouth and may even stick out of the mouth. Poor habitual tongue positions have been linked to headaches and **TMJ (tempomandibular joint)** pain. You may want to refer back to Activity #2 Step A to refresh your memory regarding the location of these structures. Activity #4 follows and is a wonderful way to relax before sleep or whenever you can find a bit of time to spare.

ACTIVITY #4

STRESS BUSTER COMBO (SELF-CHAKRA CONNECTION AND AUTOGENIC RELAXATION)

Time: 10 to 15 minutes

This combination of techniques is very effective for producing a calmer more PNS dominant state that enables you to tune into your body from your toes to your nose. The **Self-Chakra Connection** is one of many techniques taught by Healing Touch Program. A useful diagram outlining this technique can be found on their website at the following link:

https://www.healingtouchprogram.com/content_assets/docs/current/Self-CC-handout1.pdf

I like to use this technique in combination with "talking" to each body part while working through the exercise. Repeat phrases such as "my foot is getting warm and relaxed," or "my knee is strong and filled with calm energy" two or three times as you progress through each of the hand positions shown in the self-chakra connection diagram. This added layer is called **autogenic relaxation** and it too is a very useful way of reducing your stress and becoming more in tune with your body. You might also ask each a few body parts what it is they would like you to know. Remember to keep your breathing deep and slow throughout this exercise for added relaxation.

Reflective Space for Stress Buster Combo.

PART 2

THE ENERGY OF
YOUR HEART

*"A new idea is first condemned as ridiculous and then dismissed
as trivial, until finally, it becomes what everybody knows."*
—**William James**

Overview

Since the dawn of time, mystics, philosophers, and theologians have sought
to understand and explain who we are and how the universe works. The
above quotation by James sets the stage for Part 2 wherein the forces
and energies that give form to the world are explored. Energies such as
electricity, magnetism, light and sound are not limited to the physics
of the day-to-day world and are intimately involved with all aspects of
your existence. An existence that extends from the furthest reaches of the
universe to the minute pulses of energy contained within the atom.

Humans are equipped with an incredible set of sensory organs enabling
them to perceive some of these energies. Despite individual differences,
humans often believe others see and hear things in the same manner.
Even shared experiences however, are frequently complicated by different
perceptions or reactions to an event. For example, you and a friend may

be travelling in the same car when you are hit by another vehicle. If you were distracted or daydreaming it may have shocked you as it seemed to have come out of nowhere. Your friend on the other hand, was more alert and saw the vehicle head straight for you. Current thoughts, feelings, and past events temper your reaction and can range from traumatic to trifling. Witnesses often put another spin on an accident and what you think happened isn't what everyone else saw.

Different perspectives provide different experiences and so in the broader scheme of things, the question becomes, " how do you really know what you know?" Part 2 explores this theme through the lenses of science, energy medicine, and the human heart.

CHAPTER 4

YOUR ELECTRICAL HEART

4:1 How do you know what you know?

"In order to define extrasensory, we need to define sensory as our knowledge of the outside world depends on our perception of it"
—Emmanuel Kant

Today, science is often used as the default setting when explanations are needed. Statements such as "it's a scientific fact" or "science has proven…" are often used to justify a point of view or opinion. Such approaches presume the information gleaned via scientific research is above reproach. It is crucial to remember science is a human invention and its methods are not new! Galileo Galilei (1564-1642) is considered the "father" of scientific methodology, although glimmers of this protocol can be found as far back as ancient Greece. Many incredible discoveries have been the gifts of scientific rigor yet all scientific work is human by design.

In *"The Intention Experiments"* Lynne McTaggart cites significant evidence indicating the assumptions and intentions of a researcher can alter the outcome of an experiment. The following excerpt of Jan Baptista van

Helmont's work conducted circa 1648 is an intriguing historical example of how assumptions can falsify "scientific facts":

"That all plants immediately and substantially stem from the element water alone I have learnt from the following experiment. I took an earthern vessel in which I placed two hundred pounds of earth dried in an oven, and watered with rainwater. I planted in it a willow tree weighing five pounds. Five years later it had developed a tree weighing one hundred and sixty-nine pounds and about three ounces. Nothing but rain (or distilled water) had been added. The large vessel was placed in earth and covered by an iron lid with a tin-surface that was pierced with many holes. I have not weighed the leaves that came off in the four autumn seasons. Finally I dried the earth in the vessel again and found the same two hundred pounds of it diminished by about two ounces. Hence one hundred and sixty-four pounds of wood, bark and roots had come up from water alone."

Although van Helmont's experimental design and the accuracy of the data are sound his assumption that nothing else of significance could have entered the vessels seems naïve today. One hundred years would pass before Antoine Lavoisier (1743-1794) demonstrated the existence of carbon dioxide and oxygen gas along with their pivotal roles in photosynthesis and respiration. Lavoisier's discoveries and innovative brilliance was considered heretical at the time. He was guillotined in 1794 during the French Revolution for his work--work that is still a cornerstone of modern chemistry.

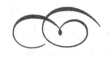

ACTIVITY #5

EXPLORING YOUR ASSUMPTIONS

Time: 15 minutes

Objectives: Exploring your assumptions is a useful avenue for personal growth and awareness. It acts as a window into helping you to understand and process the origins of your thoughts and ideas. Additionally, it acts as a creative tool to help you "think outside the box". Activity # 5 is intended as such a tool and invites you to investigate what you believe and why.

1. The first step towards understanding the dance between energy and you is to begin with you. Take a few minutes to brainstorm and write down as many of your personal assumptions and beliefs that come to mind. The general categories are physical, emotional, mental and spiritual (**PEMS**). Some items may overlap which is okay e.g. beside "physical self" you might say you are healthy and this may spill over into the emotional or mental categories. If you have no belief or assumptions for a section consider this as information as well.

2. Once you have completed the column on your assumptions, take a moment to consider how or why you hold that particular belief. This may include comments such as: "everybody knows …", "I read it in a newspaper," "its common sense" and so on. You may also want to speculate upon the origins of how you know things.

Are your beliefs primarily family truths, urban myths, scientific, or secular?

3. When you have filled in the second column take some time to reflect upon the big picture. What do you normally base these assumptions upon? Are your self-assessments positive or negative? What would you like to change or improve? Describe some strategies you might use to make these changes. Record these and any other thoughts that come to mind in the chart or the reflective space below.

Assumptions/Beliefs   **How you know this?**

Physical Self:

Emotional Self:

Mental Self:

Spiritual Self:

Reflective space for Activity # 5:

As the rigor of scientific inquiry permeated Western thought it became essential to back up one's point of view with solid research. The backlash of this process was that it marginalized and negated any intuitive understanding of nature and the universe. Paradoxically, as discoveries on the frontiers of subtle energy now gain acceptance, scientists are developing the tools to measure and explain the same phenomena they once suppressed. For example, oscillating magnetic fields are being developed for the treatment of damaged bone, nerve, skin and ligaments. These fields are identical to the pulsating **bio-magnetic** fields emanating from the hands of trained energy therapists. According to James Oschman (2000)

> *"We now know that the living organism is designed both to adapt to and utilize many different kinds of forces, and that healing processes involve the operation of many kinds of communications. There is no single "life force" or "healing energy". Instead there are many systems in the body that conduct various kinds of energy and information from place to place. Different energy therapies focus on different aspects of this multiplicity, and each set of these therapies presents a valuable set of clues and testable hypotheses about how human energy systems work. The physiological and anatomical systems in the body and the energy systems interdigitate. Effective therapeutic work on one system inevitably affects the composite."*

Ideally, bridging scientific and esoteric wisdom develops a rich multidisciplinary perspective of yourself and this world. Prior to discussing the nature of bio-fields and their interactions, it is useful to revisit early discoveries linking electricity and magnetism with living things. Such inquiries lead to new ways of thinking about energy and the nature of matter.

4.2 Frog's Legs and You

> *"Animal electricity is the essence of life itself."*
> **—Luigi Galvani**

One evening, many years ago, my in-laws took us out for dinner to a lovely French restaurant known for its haute cuisine. My first husband often teased his mother, and knowing she was horrified of frog's legs brashly ordered them. When I asked her why she disliked them, she told me that some time ago she had been at a formal banquet and was served frog's legs. Naively, she cut into the meat, and the leg jumped off the plate. Startled, she screamed and bolted up from the table scattering her dinner in the process. She was so embarrassed as the waiters scurried to clean up the mess that she vowed never to eat frog's legs again. Just as she finished her story, as if on cue, my husband was served his appetizer and cut into them with a flourish. While he was raving about how good they tasted, one of the legs' jumped off his plate! We all laughed so hard we could barely eat our dinner!

Frog's legs have been jumping off dinner plates for several hundred years and the spectacle was often blamed on undercooked meat. At the time, I remembered a physiology lab where changes in the electrical activity of frog's legs were recorded as they contracted but I was laughing too much to mention it. Fortunately, an Italian by the name of Luigi Galvani not only noticed but, chose to investigate this phenomenon.

In the 1780's, at the University of Bolonga, Galvani performed experiments with electric charges on frogs. He found that when he applied an electric current to the spinal cord of the frog, it would generate contractions throughout its body. One day, the exposed **sciatic nerve** of a frog's leg was touched with a charged metal scalpel. Everyone was startled as the frog's leg kicked even though it was no longer attached to its body. Intrigued, Galvani discovered the frog's leg would twitch when two different metals e.g. copper and silver wires, touched the nerve simultaneously.

During this time, a mysterious substance transmitted by metals called electricity was discovered. Galvani proposed that some kind of "animal electricity" was secreted by the body and flowed through the metal knife to activate the frog's muscle contractions. His research established the importance of nerves as a type of electrical conductor designed to carry information through the body. His work contradicted the popular model of "water channels" as proposed by his contemporary Descartes and much scientific debate ensued. Galvani's work eventually led to research on how biological systems control the flow of ions (charged particles) to enable nerves and other tissues to transmit electrical signals. Thus an entirely new field of research—**electrophysiology**—was born.

Evidence supporting Galvani's theories had to wait until the technology to detect and measure these tiny, electric exchanges was developed. Today, it is well known how the largest electrical impulses flow via nerves. Ongoing discoveries regarding subtle electrical impulses in all of your organs, tissues and cells is revealing sophisticated networks throughout your body. Before we can explore this in greater depth, let's first delve into the nature of electricity.

4.3 Electricity and You

> *"Chemical affinity and electricity are one in the same."*
> —**Michael Faraday**

As a child, you may recall the immense fun you had at parties rubbing your hair with a balloon and getting it to stick to the wall or combing your hair with a plastic comb and having it fly out all over the place. Nor can you forget the shocking experience of touching a doorknob after scuffing your feet thru a carpet. Descriptions of similar phenomena date back to ancient Greece including the creation of invisible forces by rubbing amber (petrified tree resin) with a piece of wool. The Greek word for amber is *elecktron* so this effect became known as an electron charge.

Rubbing a glass rod with cotton was also observed to produce a force. It was considered a different force because the charged glass rod attracted a charged amber rod and vice versa as shown in **Fig. 9**. In addition, two rods with the same charge repelled one another. In the mid 1700's, Benjamin Franklin named the charge on the glass rod positive while the charge on the amber rod was called negative. He stated that *like charges attract and unlike charges repel*. Although it was not understood how or why these phenomena occurred, there seemed to be a link between electric charges and matter.

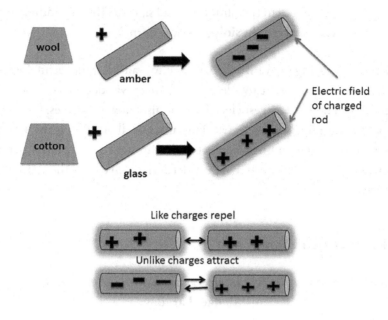

Fig. 9 Basic Electrostatics and the production of Electric Fields

Franklin's studies included his famous experiment where he flew a kite during a lightning storm. The kite was attached to a metal wire connected to a container used for collecting electrical charges called a Leyden jar. When lightning struck the kite, the jar became charged. Upon touching the jar, Franklin received an electric shock and demonstrated a link between the charges generated by friction and that of lightning. The generation of lightning was later explained as a build up of a static electrical charge caused by the movement of large masses of air. When charge differences reached a critical point, the accumulated charge would move or jump; which was observed as lightning.

In the mid 1800's, scientists were fascinated when they found electrical forces of attraction and repulsion could act through a distance. Michael Faraday defined the region of space around an electric charge that could transmit this force as a **field** (Fig. 9). The strength of an electric field depends upon the source and decreases with the distance from the source. Lightning for example, produces very strong fields and these scattered explosions of electricity pump energy into the outer layers of our atmosphere, particularly the **ionosphere.** An estimated 200 lightning strikes occur every second. They produce standing waves of energy in our atmosphere and generate significant electrical and magnetic fields. Exciting research has revealed the frequencies of the fields in the ionosphere parallel those produced by your heart and brain. Intriguing links between human behavior and atmospheric phenomena have been discovered and are currently under investigation.

Further insights between electricity and matter resulted from the experiments of Alessandro Volta--a contemporary of Galvani. Volta constructed a *sandwich* from two different metal discs e.g. zinc and copper as shown in **Fig. 10.** Individual wires ran from each metal disc, which were separated from each other by a *filling* of blotting paper soaked in salt water. When the wires from each metal touched they produced a spark. Further research showed that the intensity of the spark varied with the choice of metals and the number of sandwiches in the stack. Volta had discovered how to produce a steady flow of electrons or electricity without using friction to build up a static charge e.g. rubbing amber with wool. His stacks of metal sandwiches became known as **voltaic piles**.

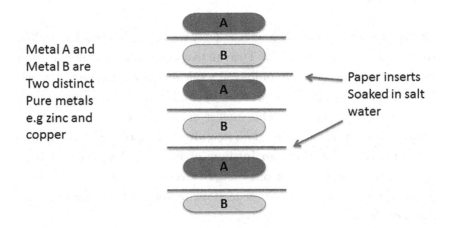

Metal A and
Metal B are
Two distinct
Pure metals
e.g zinc and
copper

Paper inserts
Soaked in salt
water

Fig. 10 Simplified Diagram of a Voltaic Pile

Just as water needs pressure to flow through a hose, electricity requires a *push*. The term **voltage (v)** describes the amount of *"push"* forcing electricity through a system. Volta's stack became known as the **voltaic pile** and enabled scientists to produce and control an electrical charge travelling in one direction called **direct current** (**DC**). A new age in engineering and technology had begun. Even more exciting was the discovery that DC current could be used to decompose water into hydrogen and oxygen revealing the electrical nature of the chemical bond.

A surge of discoveries followed Volta's work and it became apparent that a competition for electrons existed amongst metals. Like a tug of war, they were ranked by their ability to pull electrons from one another. Precious metals such as gold and platinum are the strongest while metals like iron and zinc lose their electrons more easily and are readily corroded. An early version of this hierarchy was called the **Activity Series.** Later it was expanded to include many other substances and was developed into a standardized table of reduction potentials or E^0 values. These tables can be found in most chemistry textbooks and became an important tool for predicting the ease with which a reaction might take place. Many advances in electrochemistry including the development of solar panels and lightweight batteries for cell phones have evolved from the information found in these tables.

The use of electricity to light homes and city streets began in the late 1800's. At that time, direct current (DC) was all that was available. Unfortunately, its ability to illuminate light bulbs was weak and inefficient. Furthermore, it could not be transported more than two miles without needing a power boost. Enter Nikola Tesla who forever changed the way in which we utilize electricity. He introduced his new **alternating current** (**AC**) system of electricity to the American Institute of Electrical Engineers in 1888 and laid the foundation for our modern electrical systems. Tesla's work included over forty patents for generators, motors and transformers—all based on AC and still in use today.

Tesla also loved to entertain and was renowned for exciting demonstrations of his latest experiments at his parties including that of the **human energy field** (**HEF**) or **aura**. His discoveries about electric and magnetic fields remain profound and it is now known that all living things generate electrical and magnetic fields. Subtle and elusive, these fields are emerging as crucial players in the maintenance of your health and wellness. To this end, section **5.8** is dedicated to the emerging work on energy fields with special attention to that of your heart.

When you consider all the incredible inventions that have occurred in the last 150 years or so, you might wonder why it took so long to detect the existence of electricity in living organisms. The main reason is the incredibly subtle nature of these electric currents and the lack of tools capable of such delicate measurements. To establish a baseline let's look at the use and measurement of electricity in your home and then compare it to your nervous system. A typical household outlet in North America for example, delivers one **ampere (I)** or 6.24×10^{18} units of electrical charge per second. The push behind this delivery is 110 volts; which is more than enough to knock you over and a give you a severe electrical burn.

Living organisms, in contrast, register very tiny changes in electrical potential. These values are so small they must be measured in micro units. One microvolt for example, is one millionth ($1/1,000,000^{th}$) the strength of one volt. Detection of such minute electrical signals; was pioneered by Raymond Saxton Burr in the 1930's. A professor of Anatomy at Yale University, Burr developed a tool called the **vacuum tube micro voltmeter.** He used this device to study electrical changes in the sciatic nerve of frogs' legs-- almost 150 years after Galvani's discoveries. Typically, an impulse in a motor nerve is measured at 0.2 microamperes and 70 microvolts. This means the amperage and voltage are about 10 million times smaller than that used in a household. No wonder it took so long to discover the electrical nature of life let alone imagine its' existence!

Much of traditional biology and physiology including the generation of your heartbeat is based on early ideas regarding the structure of atoms and ions (**4.6**). Before delving further into the modern implications of Burr's research, a conceptual review of what everybody thinks they know about atoms is needed to set the stage for the upheaval quantum physics brings to the biology of all living things including yourself!

4.4 Atoms and Elements—the Basics

"The crucial step was to write down elements in terms of their atoms...I don't know how they could do chemistry beforehand, it didn't make any sense."
—Sir Henry Kroto

Some of humankind's earliest connections with the elements are linked to metals. Copper beads dating from 6000 BC have been found in artifacts from the Middle East. Items of lead, gold, silver and iron have been uncovered in other archeological sites, some as old as 4000 BC. Metals have always been treasured for their shiny luster, malleability, and conductivity. Precious metals like silver and gold also resist corrosion; which adds to their value. The fascination with metals (and wealth) was so great that from 400 to 1400 AD alchemists explored the mysteries of nature in order to turn base metals, such as lead, into gold.

Until the late 1700's, little was known about the other elements. Air for example, was known as *ether* and considered to be an essence infusing the realms of the Gods. Enter John Dalton;. He conducted hundreds of experiments and kept meticulous records of changes in mass, pressure, temperature and volume for each one. His research led to groundbreaking discoveries of basic chemical laws including:

- Air is a mixture of different gases including oxygen, carbon dioxide, and nitrogen.
- Pure substances combine in specific whole number ratios e.g. water is, 1 part oxygen to 2 parts hydrogen (H_2O) while carbon dioxide is 1 part carbon to 2 parts oxygen (CO_2).
- Each gas, in any mixture e.g. air, acts independently of the others

In order to explain the results of his experiments, he developed a theory; which became Dalton's Atomic Theory. In this theory he proposed:

- All matter was made from indivisible building blocks called **atoms**
- A substance made from only one type of atom was an **element**
- Elements combined in **definite proportions** in a chemical reaction

Although innovative, Dalton's model did not encompass the electrical nature of matter—something was missing! Nearly one hundred years later, two physicists; Ernest Rutherford and Niels Bohr designed such a model. Basics of their model, is what you were taught in junior science and how most people still envision an atom. This simplified view consists of a dense center (**nucleus**) occupied by two types of particles i.e. positive (**protons**) and neutral (**neutrons**). Negative particles-**electrons**- are found outside the nucleus and organized into energy levels originally thought of as rings. Early diagrams of atoms thus resemble a solar system. A few examples are shown in **Fig. 11.**

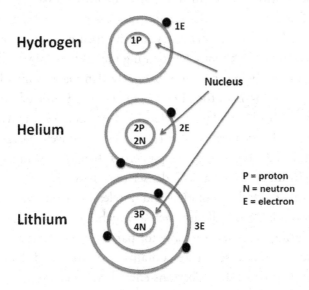

Fig. 11 Rutherford-Bohr models for the Atoms of the First Three Elements: Hydrogen, Helium and Lithium

While useful for introducing chemical bonding and reactions this model is misleading because it leads to a fixed, mechanical view of matter. Atoms are not like that! The stars are giant cauldrons for the creation of new atoms through a process called nuclear fusion. Here, protons, neutrons, and electrons are engaged in an energy dance as they jostle one another and to achieve stable energy arrangements. Changes in the proportions of these particles, changes the identity of the atom. For example, when another proton is added to the nucleus, it's positive charge increases and it attracts another electron--a new atom is the result. Although changes in the atomic structure are invisible to the naked eye, changes in the physical and chemical properties such as color, density, and reactivity are not and enable scientists to distinguish substances.

The number of protons in the nucleus of an element is called its **atomic number** and it largely pre-determines the characteristics of an element. Let's look more closely at this relationship by comparing the properties of the first three elements as follows:

1. **Hydrogen**: an atom of hydrogen (H) consists of one proton and one electron. The element exists in nature as a pair of atoms (H_2) and is a colorless, odorless and tasteless gas at room temperature. It's lighter than air buoyancy and inexpensive ease of production, made it the first choice for inflating the giant airships of the 1930's. However, hydrogen is also extremely flammable which led to the tragic explosion of the Hindenberg and the demise of airships. The ease with which it loses an electron determines its reactivity as well. When this occurs, hydrogen becomes a positively charged particle (H^{+1}), and has very different properties than its elemental form.

2. **Helium:** although a little denser than hydrogen, it is still lighter than air, odorless, colorless and tasteless. In contrast to hydrogen, helium is chemically unreactive which it a much safer choice for inflating balloons especially for parties. It exists as a single atom and its atomic structure contains 2 protons and 2 neutrons in the nucleus while 2 electrons encircle the nucleus. This forms an extremely stable pattern therefore helium belongs to the chemical family of unreactive or **inert** elements.

3. **Lithium** contains one proton and one electron more than helium. Its properties are different too. Lithium is a silvery, soft metal that reacts vigorously with water releasing heat and huge amounts of hydrogen gas. An explosive mixture is formed in the process. During the reaction with water, lithium loses its outer electron and becomes a Li^{+1} ion whose properties are distinctly different from its nature as an element.

I still find it fascinating how a slight shift in the number of protons or electrons creates an entirely different species. Revolutionary in its concepts, the Rutherford-Bohr model provided a glimpse into the mysteries underlying the behavior of matter and a crucial springboard for what was to become the quantum model of the atom--the theme of **5.4** and **5.5**.

The search for underlying patterns is a common pursuit amongst scientists including Dimitri Mendeleev. Accordingly, he noticed how some elements displayed similarities in their physcial properties and chemical reactivity. In 1869, he wrote the properties of the known elements on separate cards and via frequent shuffling and rearranging of the cards he was able to organize them into **chemical families** based on their similarities. His work led to the development of an early version of The Periodic Table of the Elements. Today's table is a brilliant organizer of all the known elements, their properties, and much more! A simple outline of the table is shown in **Fig.12**.

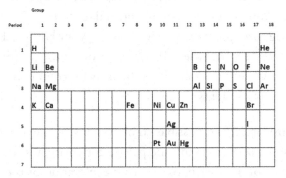

Periods (rows) are numbered 1 through 7 and correspond to the number of energy levels available to the elements in that row.
Groups (columns) are numbered 1 through 18 and represent an increase in the number of protons in the nucleus from left to right within each row.
Chemical families occur when elements in the same group have similar chemical properties e.g. group 17 is the halogen family.

Fig. 12 Outline of the Modern Periodic Table of the Elements showing the location of selected elements

As shown in **Fig. 12**, the elements are organized in order of increasing atomic number from left to right and top to bottom. Chemical families are clustered into columns and many interesting patterns emerge from this arrangement. One of them is the grouping of **metals** on the left side of the table and **non-metals** on the right. The properties of metals were discussed previously in **4.3** however, is important to remember that metals compete for electrons and stronger metals take electrons from weaker ones resisting corrosion in the process.

61

In contrast, non-metals are mostly insulators of heat and electricity and range from gases, to dull, brittle solids. The far right column begins with helium and features the family of inert gases. Next door, beginning with fluorine, is a very reactive group known as the halogen family. They are extremely good at ripping electrons from other elements—often violently as in the case of explosives. When non-metals gain electrons, they acquire a negative charge. This makes them very attractive to species with positive charges and results in an **ionic** bond. Such bonds are typically very strong and ionic substances—broadly known as salts-- have high melting points e.g. sodium chloride (table salt) melts at 801 degrees Celsius. (A diagram of sodium chloride is included as part of **Fig. 13** in the next section.)

Who would have guessed the subtle differences in electronic structure between metals and non-metals would be responsible for the formation of charged species? Known as ions, they are integral to the transfer of electrical messages flowing through the tissues and cells of your body including the activation of your heart muscles. The next section (**4.7**) introduces, the importance of water and the role played by **ions** for conducting electrical information in living systems.

When you consider all the possible combinations of the 118 (or more) elements, there is a seemingly infinite palette for creation in the material world but that is for another book. Further exploration of the elements, their properties and the incredible variety of compounds they form can be glimpsed through the following interactive websites.

The first of the links listed is to a colorful, basic table while the second one is more academic.

http://elements.wlonk.com/index.htm

www.rsc.org/**periodic-table**

4.5 Ions, Electrolytes and You

> *"... it is electricity that kicks a cell into life. This electricity is intelligent; it carries information; it has Qi (pronounced "chi"); it is not dumb..."*
> **—Daniel Keown**

Our physical world, from an atom of hydrogen to a human being, is a highly structured organization of energy. Ancients devoted much of their lives to finding the "philosopher's stone"--a magical catalyst to transmute other substances into gold. Today, nuclear physicists are capable of transmuting one element into another by altering the energy within the atom. If the addition or subtraction of electrons and protons can create entirely different elements, then electrical signals, however subtle, must impact life. The question then becomes how are these subtle signals transmitted?

Water is a major component of your entire body. It is found in every cell, and all of the fluids; which permeate your tissues and organs. These fluids are like an organic soup and contain many substances including charged particles called ions. Ions carry minute electrical signals in and out of cells or along nerves and muscles.

Earlier it was mentioned that Volta's electrochemical cell only worked when the blotting paper was soaked with salt water. At the time, it was a mystery but now it can be explained. When a salt dissolves in water, its chemical bonds are broken to form positive and negative ions in the solution. These ions are called **electrolytes**. When an external electric potential is applied, they migrate through the solution towards an electrode with the opposite charge. The movement of the ions completes the circuit and the transfer of an electric charge in this manner is known an **electrolytic conduction**. **Fig, 13** illustrates this process using table salt as an example.

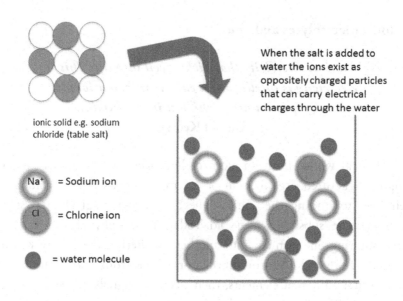

When the salt is added to water the ions exist as oppositely charged particles that can carry electrical charges through the water

ionic solid e.g. sodium chloride (table salt)

Na^+ = Sodium ion

Cl = Chlorine ion

= water molecule

Fig. 13 The Formation of Electrolytes by Dissolving an Ionic Solid in Water.

When the breaking of ionic bonds occurs by dissolving a salt in water the ions are free to move towards an opposite electrical charge. This process enables to electrolytic conduction whether it is in a beaker, the ocean or your body.

The presence of ions in your body fluids facilitate the transmission of millions of subtle electrical messages and hence form a subtle network of electrical signals that extend from head to toe. All cells contain ion pumps in their membranes to generate the electric potentials that are crucial to health and wellness. Just as Galvani glimpsed so many years ago, you are filled with **bioelectricity.**

An elegant example of bioelectricity is the transmission of a message through a motor neuron as illustrated in **Figs. 14** and **15.** The main body (**soma**) of the cell contains the **nucleus** while fine filaments known as **dendrites** receive the stimulus. When received, a signal is passed down a long slender part of the nerve called the **axon.** It leapfrogs down the length of the nerve as sodium (Na^{+1}) ions are rapidly pumped into and then out of the cell. This process creates minute cyclic changes in the electric potential of the cell membrane and serves to transmit the signal. At the end of the axon, tiny sacs in the cell are stimulated to secrete a chemical. This chemical carries the message across a minute gap called the **synapse** to its intended destination. The neurotransmitter, acetylcholine, as discussed in **2.4**, is an example of such a chemical signal.

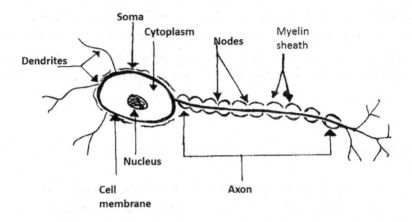

Fig. 14 Diagram of a Motor Neuron

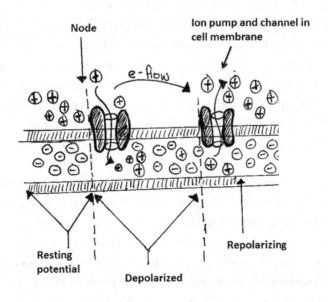

Fig. 15 Signal Transmission along the Axon of a Motor Neuron

As most athletes are aware, optimal performance is maintained by staying hydrated and preserving your electrolyte balance. This balance becomes increasingly important when there is extensive water loss or retention. Certain medications, excessive perspiration, diarrhea, vomiting, and poor kidney function all contribute to dehydration and electrolyte imbalances. When your electrolytes especially sodium (Na^{+1}) potassium (K^{+1}), and calcium (Ca^{+2}) ions, are out of balance, signals become scrambled and muscles cannot recover properly. This not only affects strength and coordination, it can severely impact your heart. Section **4.8** explores the patterns of electrical coordination that comprise your heartbeat--all mediated by electrolytes.

4.6 You and Your ECG

> *"It is much more important to know what sort of a patient has a disease than what sort of a disease a patient has"*
> **—William Osler**

As mentioned in **1.1** your embryonic heart began beating at 3 weeks. Later on in Chapter 2, the focus was on tuning into how your heartbeat responds to changes in physical activity, thoughts, emotions etc. This section builds upon this awareness as it examines the patterns of electrical signals generated by your heartbeat. This is known as an **electrocardiogram (ECG)**. There have been some exciting discoveries about these patterns and the insights they provide with respect to your health and wellness. We will begin with a snapshot of how electrical impulses are transmitted by your heart and the manner in which your heart muscle responds.

Cardiac muscle is unique type of muscle stimulated by specialized nerve cells. Before it contracts, a large number of positive ions (magnesium, sodium, potassium, and calcium) flow across the membranes of the heart muscles creating an electric current; which stimulates contraction. This creates a pattern of electrical waves corresponding to the **depolarization** and **repolarization** of your heart muscle. Although relatively weak, these signals are readily transmitted by the electrolytes in your blood and lymph and can be detected anywhere on the surface of your body. Stimulated heart muscle contracts in a cyclic manner as described in **1.3**. The cycle begins with the SA node and sends out a ripple of changes in the electrical potential throughout your heart.

In 1906, Willem Einthoven, a Professor of Physiology at the University of Leiden, discovered that every cycle of your heartbeat is accompanied by waves of electrical activity. Moreover, these electrical waves are not restricted to your heart and actually reverberate throughout your entire body. Working with his son, an electrical engineer, Einthoven succeeded in designing a device to record your heart's electrical fluctuations.

His invention consisted of a very long (several meters) silver-coated quartz filament of an almost microscopic diameter and negligible mass. **Electromagnets** were positioned on either side of this filament and caused sideways movement of the filament to vary in proportion to the amount of electrical current. Movement of the filament was heavily magnified and projected onto a moving photographic plate. Using this sensitive device, Einthoven was able to record potential changes of frequencies in the order of 100,000 times per second.

Over the years, techniques for recording the heart's electrical activity evolved into the ECG. Today it provides significant insights into the function and vitality of your heart. Typically, an ECG (**Fig.16**) displays a pattern of peaks and valleys with the following three main components:

1. **P** wave: occurs as the atria begin to contract and represent the current produced as they depolarize in preparation for the next contraction.
2. **QRS** complex: generated as the ventricles start to contract. It is a hybrid of three separate waves of depolarization running through the ventricles i.e. the Q, R, and S waves.
3. **T** wave: represents the recovery of the ventricles from their contraction--hence it is a repolarization wave. (N.B. Repolarization of the atria is overshadowed by the QRS complex and usually goes undetected).

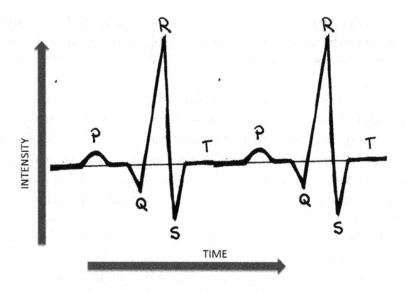

**Fig. 16 Simplified Diagram of an ECG
indicating the P, QRS, and T waves**

The time from one P wave to the next represents one cycle of your heartbeat. Therefore, your heart rate equals the number of P waves per minute. Originally, the musical speed *Moderato* was based on the average heart rate of 72 beats/min. However, this implies that the time between P waves has the precision of a metronome; which is not the case. Most people have some variation in the time interval between heartbeats. This is called **Heart Rate Variability (HRV)**.

An ECG is considered the most effective tool for monitoring HRV although taking a pulse or measuring blood pressure can also be useful. Connes (2010) found that regardless of age, health, and/or fitness level daily physical activity has a strong positive impact on your HRV. HRV measurements provide a window into the autonomic nervous system and the nervous system in general. Significant research on this topic conducted by the Heart Math Institute has led to an idea called Heart Rate Coherence. (More details on this can be found in **7.1**)

Einthoven received the Nobel Prize for his work in 1924, and the ECG still stands as a profound diagnostic tool for the heart. An ECG records the electrical efficiency of heart muscle and is used to detect different types of heart disease e.g. valve malfunction, arrhythmias, and various hypertrophies. It is fascinating to note Einthoven discovered each ECG has a unique electrical signature and, just like fingerprints, your ECG can be used to identify you.

Simply put, your physical heart is so much more than a mechanical pump. It is an electrochemical generator suspended in an electrolytic solution in the core of your body. It sends electrical signals that transmit an incredible array of information throughout your body. What they are and their significance will be presented in the upcoming chapters—stay tuned!

CHAPTER 5

YOUR HEART'S FIELD

5.1 Light and You

> *"When you change the way you look at things,*
> *the things you look at change"*
> **—Max Planck**

Most of us are captivated by the magic of rainbows whether they arc over the sky or dance on the wall as sunlight passes through a prism. The fascinating patterns of light and color you can create with mirrors and lenses never failed to transform a rowdy junior science class into one of excited whispers. Watching their enchantment was always delightful and evoked memories of the Walt Disney movie "Pollyanna". In one scene, Pollyanna visits an unhappy invalid convalescing in her darkened bedroom. Boldly, she opens all the curtains and starts to hang prisms in the windows. As they illuminate the room, the woman complains the light is bothersome. Unperturbed, Pollyanna continues to suspend the prisms and as the room fills with rainbows, the woman's mood shifts to outbursts of sheer delight.

Light is such an integral part of daily life that it is often taken for granted until you witness a spectacular display of lightning or fireworks. We associate light with vision and understanding thru phrases such as " the light turned on" or "illuminating the situation" as ways of sharing our human experiences. The absence of light--especially in the winter months—affects some people so severely that they become depressed or **SAD (Seasonal Affective Disorder)**. What is light and why is an understanding of its behavior important to you and your heart? Chapter 5 addresses these questions and more. It begins with the early debates about the nature of light and evolves into the discoveries that defined its electromagnetic and quantum behavior. The implications of this research and its impact upon our understanding of matter and life are then discussed. The chapter concludes with how living organisms generate bio-fields and why an understanding of your heart's bio-field is especially vital to your own health and wellness.

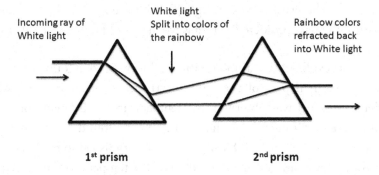

Fig. 17 Diagram of White Light passing in sequence through two Prisms

The nature of light was controversial for hundreds of years. At one time, color was thought to be a mixture of light and dark while prisms were believed to color white light. This idea originated from what seems to happen when you observe a ray of light travelling through a prism. The first prism in **Fig. 17** shows how the light ray bends slightly as it passes from the air into the glass and a thin wedge of color becomes visible inside the prism. When the ray passes from the glass back into the air this process is repeated, widening the wedge of color even more to display the colors of the rainbow.

In 1668, **Isaac Newton** focused the rainbow produced by one prism through another prism and to everyone's surprise the rainbow returned to white light. In other words, a prism was just as capable of re-assembling a rainbow into white light as it was of breaking white light into a rainbow. This is shown in the second prism in **Fig. 17.** His experiment was important in that he showed white light itself contained all the colors.

Newton tried to explain the nature of light in his book *Opticks*. Based on its ability to travel in straight lines e.g. the visible path followed by the beam of a flashlight in the dark, he proposed that light was made of particles. Others such as, Christian Huygens believed light was a wave that travelled through a material called the *ether*. Whether light was a particle or a wave was hotly debated until Thomas Young conducted his famous double slit experiments in 1801. His results provided such convincing evidence for the wave nature of light that by the end of the nineteenth century, light was considered to be a wave that could travel through space.

As scientists explored the rainbow, visible colors were soon found to occupy only a very small part of the light spectrum. It began in 1801 when William Herschel was observing the temperature of different colors. As he moved a thermometer through a rainbow, he found the temperature increased from violet to red. However, he was astonished to find that as he moved the thermometer past the red zone, the temperature increased yet again. He correctly assumed there was some type of invisible light beyond the red zone, a type of light known as heat or **infrared** (**IR**) (see **Fig. 18**).

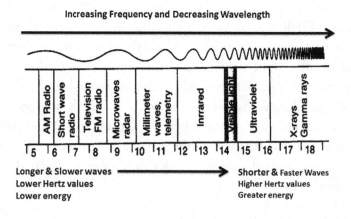

Fig. 18 Basics of the Electromagnetic Spectrum

Sunlight and fires are common sources of infrared. As a substance absorbs heat the particles gain energy and are stimulated to vibrate and move with greater force. As this happens, the substance gets hot and is considered to be increasing its kinetic energy. Changes in the phases of matter result from absorption or release of IR e.g. heating ice increases the movement of the particles and produces water. As it cools, it loses heat energy and the water molecules slow down and move closer together until they form ice. Such experiments link heat energy to the movement of particles (**kinetic energy**). Your body is constantly releasing heat energy (IR); which is why night someone using night vision goggles can find you in the dark!

In its early days, photographic film was based on a chemical reaction between light and silver chloride. When exposed to light, silver chloride breaks down into silver and chlorine. The more light reflected from the object, the more silver is formed and the darker the image—hence the term "negative". Shortly after the discovery of IR another scientist, Johann Ritter was working with the effects of violet light on silver chloride. Like Herschel, Ritter noticed seemingly invisible rays beyond the violet range. These rays increased the speed of the chemical reaction even more than violet light and were named **ultraviolet (UV).**

Roughly ten percent of the UV you receive is from the sun while other sources include arc welding, and mercury vapor lamps. Just as plants use light to stimulate photosynthesis, your body uses light, specifically UV, to produce **Vitamin D**. Exposure to UV activates a substance in your skin (**7-dehydrocholestero**l); which produces an inactive form of Vitamin D. This is stored in your liver and kidneys until needed at which time your body converts it to Vitamin D (**calcitriol**). Hollick (2010), has shown that lack of sunlight and Vitamin D deficiencies result in:

- poor absorption of minerals such as calcium and iron
- increased risk of heart attacks and heart disease
- weakened immune system
- increased inflammation.

Additionally, certain chemical bonds in DNA and other molecules of life can be altered by exposure to excess UV. Apparently, light is not used just for photosynthesis and Vitamin D production, it interacts with all living organisms at the molecular level. Not only does the sun illuminate your physical world, it is crucial for your existence.

Rays of light-- some visible, some not—only hint at the deeper mystery. In 1845, Michael Faraday discovered that light rays travelling in the same plane (**polarized**) respond to magnets. At that time however, light, electricity and magnetism were perceived as distinctly separate phenomena until James Clerk Maxwell decided to explore the possibility of their interconnections. During the 1860's, he developed a series of equations proving the existence of an **electromagnetic** field.

Maxwell's ideas were revolutionary! Four equations were created to describe this field. Two of these equations predicted the existence and behavior of waves within this field. Additionally, his calculations revealed these waves must travel at the speed of light "c" (3.00×10^8 m/sec). His equations demonstrated that light contained both electric and magnetic properties and therefore concluded light existed as an electromagnetic wave.

Eventually, it became apparent that each frequency of light was only a very tiny portion of an infinite spectrum. A chart of the **electromagnetic spectrum** as shown in **Fig. 18**, was designed to organize this body of knowledge. Visible light (400 to 700 nm) is located near the middle of this chart while infrared (1 mm to 750 nm) is left of visible light. The wavelengths become increasingly longer as you move to the left and when they reach 187-10 mm they are classified as **microwaves.**

Maxwell also predicted an electrical circuit could be used to produce very long waves of light. This was achieved by Heinrich Hertz in 1887. Using a **spark gap apparatus**—similar to a spark plug—Hertz was able to make an electric charge rush back and forth to produce long invisible waves travelling at the speed of light— **radio waves**! Radio waves (0.187 m to 600 m) can be as long as 3 football fields and Hertz essentially paved the way for today's abundant wireless communication. The longest wavelengths, **ELF** waves (100,000 m to 10,000 km)--often produced by lightning strikes—are at the left of this spectrum and considered to have the least amount of energy in the spectrum.

Moving to the right of visible light in Fig. 18, the waves become increasingly shorter. **Ultraviolet waves** (400 to 10 nm) are just past violet light. As the wavelengths continue to decrease, they possess more energy and ultimately produce **ionizing radiation**. This type of radiation is capable of breaking chemical bonds and penetrating matter. **X-rays** (10 to 0.01 nm) were the first in this region to be discovered. Mostly man-made, they are used for imaging your bones and teeth. **Gamma rays**, are the most damaging and have the shortest wavelength--less than 0.01 nm—roughly the size of an atomic nucleus. Nuclear reactions occurring in our sun and other stars produce gamma rays.

A video tour and great graphics of the EM spectrum can be found at the following websites:

http://missionscience.nasa.gov/ems/emsVideo_01intro.html

https://en.wikipedia.org/wiki/Electromagnetic_radiation

As often happens with a new discovery, the development of the EM spectrum raised more questions than it answered. Intensive studies of light, magnetism, and electromagnetism evolved in the pursuit of answers and contributed to the development of the modern quantum model of the atom. What the quantum model means for you and your heart, will be revealed as the rest of this chapter develops.

5.2 Vibration, Frequency and You

> *"If you want to find the secrets of the universe, think*
> *in terms of energy, frequency and vibration."*
> **—Nikola Tesla**

The next part of this incredible story examines the relationship between light and energy. This exploration led to the discovery of light's quantum nature. In order to gain clarity on this research, it is important distinguish between the scientific meaning of the terms vibration and frequency. Once established, the contributions of Max Planck to the quantum atom will be discussed along with its amazing implications for the fabric of reality.

Recall from **5.1** that heating ice increased the motion of the water molecules. In this example, absorption of heat (IR) energy makes the water molecules physically move or vibrate faster. If enough energy is applied, it will reach a point where the energy is used to overcome the attractive forces holding them in place. As they break free of their solid structure, the ice melts to become a liquid—water. In this example, the application of heat increased the kinetic energy (vibration) of the water molecules. Other examples of forces that cause vibration include:

- striking a tuning fork so the prongs move back and forth or oscillate faster
- throwing a rock into a pool of water creating ripples that spread outwards in circles
- plucking a guitar string to move the string move back and forth

In each of these examples, the initial force causes movement that sends the energy outward in waves. The rings of ripples produced by throwing a rock into a body of water are perhaps the easiest to visualize. As the rock hits the water it causes the water molecules to jostle one another. This increases their vibration and transfers energy from particle to particle as the waves spread outward. The same pattern occurs amongst air particles when a guitar string or tuning fork is set in motion. Despite a similar pattern of energy transfer, you perceive these waves differently. You can see the waves in the water whereas in air you would hear the changes in pitch of the tuning fork or guitar string. Air and water both support the transfer of the energy and are examples of mediums. **Vibration** is defined as a periodic or oscillating movement. The energy that starts this movement is transferred through a medium such as water in the form of waves. The **frequency** of the waves depends upon the amount of energy being transferred.

Frequency is determined by the number of waves passing a marker in given amount of time. Imagine standing on a point of land watching waves from the water rolling onto shore. The number of waves passing by you every second, is a measure of their frequency (f). As the wavelength gets shorter, the frequency increases. So if 1 wave passes by you every second, then it's frequency is considered to be one cycle per second (cps) or 1 **hertz**. If two waves pass by every second, they would have the frequency of 2 hertz and so on.

Hertz's spark gap equipment (**5.1**) produced rapid reversals of an electric charge (+ to - and - to +). Such back and forth oscillation is an example of vibration; but in this case, it creates waves of light that spread out in three dimensions. Changing the rate of electric charge reversals changes the wavelength of the light. Light differs from other types of waves in water or air in that it does not rely upon the jostling of particles to carry its energy. This is why it can travel through space or a vacuum. Fig. 18 also shows the shortest wavelengths or highest frequencies of light have the greatest amount of energy. A good animation of how a moving electric charge across a spark gap creates light can be seen in the animation link given below.

http://www.learnerstv.com/animation/animation.php?ani=89&cat=physics

Previously, in section **5.1**, Maxwell was mentioned as having found the speed of light to be a constant (**c**). Therefore, it makes sense that if the speed of light does not change, there must be a direct relationship between the frequency (f) and wavelength (λ) of light; which can be written as:

$$c = f \text{ x}$$

speed of light = (c) frequency = (f) wavelength =(λ)

This means the shorter the wavelength the greater the frequency and vice versa.

As a consequence of this equation, short wavelength, high frequency light (e.g. x-ray) packs a bigger punch than long wave, low frequency light (e.g. radio wave). A link between energy and frequency must exist but what is it?

Enter Max Planck and his work on the radiation of energy by black bodies such as a wood stove. During his detailed experiments, Planck discovered light energy could only have a whole number i.e. 1, 2, 3, 4, 5 etc., multiplied by a constant (**h**) and by 1900, had established a direct relationship between the frequency (*f*) of light and it's energy (**E**). His equation became:

$$\mathbf{E = h \times} \mathit{f}$$

This shows the energy (**E**) of a light wave is equal to Planck's constant (**h**) times the frequency (*f*) of the wave where a value of 6.63×10^{-34} Js is assigned to Planck's constant.

Although Planck's formula explained a lot, it did not fit current theories about light. To explain his results, he proposed each frequency of light occurred in a unit or package separate from one another. He called this package a **quantum**; which means a fixed amount. Climbing stairs is a simple metaphor for this idea. You can go up 1 step or down 2 steps but there is no one-half or one quarter step in between. Planck's packaged light follows this same pattern. Each wave of light has a definite length and a specific frequency such as 1, or 2 etc., hertz. One-half or one quarter of a wave does not exist. Every frequency of light has its own fixed amount or quantum of energy therefore light is composed of energy packets.

You may find the following video of Planck's discoveries a useful explanation of this work.

https://www.britannica.com/biography/Max-Planck

Although it received very little attention at the time, Planck's idea was profound. Technically the father of quantum science, his work led to the concept of quantized energy which is fundamental to an understanding energy fields, their interactions, and the quantum model of the atom. These topics and more will evolve through the next few sections towards a fascinating look at the energy fields produced by your heart. But first, a closer look at magnetism, its relationship with electricity and the quantum model of the atom is needed.

5.3 Magnetism and You

"There is pleasure in recognizing old things from a new viewpoint."
—Richard Feynman

Ah the magic of magnets! From holding small notes on your fridge to generating electricity in hydroelectric dams, they are in use all around you. Magnets were used for healing by ancient Egyptians, Chinese and Greeks. In 1773, Mesmer began using magnets for healing and his patients frequently noticed unusual currents moving through their bodies. Mesmer soon found he could produce the same effect using his hands above the body of the patient. Research shows that every event in the human body both normal and pathological produces electrical changes and alterations in the magnetic fields about the human body. The advancement of medical diagnostic techniques and treatments such as MRI, ultrasound, electrocardiograms, electroencephalographs, and pulsed electromagnetic field therapy are all based on this paradigm.

This section starts by exploring the properties of simple magnets--some of which you may already know and then moves on to examine:

- what is known about magnetism,
- how magnets interact with electricity
- why this knowledge is significant with respect to your heart.

ACTIVITY #6

EXPERIMENTING WITH MAGNETISM

Time: 15 minutes

Objectives: This activity is meant to reacquaint you with the phenomena of magnets and magnetic fields. You will conduct simple experiments with bar magnets and your own magnetic field or aura in order sense the similarities between the two.

Part A: Get 2 magnets-- preferably bar magnets--often available in hobby or toy stores. Hold 1 magnet in each hand about ½ a meter apart with the like poles (North to North or South to South) facing each other. Slowly and gently bring the two matching poles closer together until they touch. Then slowly pull them apart again. You may repeat this several times. What happens when they are not in alignment or when you move them in circles? Just be curious and explore these interactions. You may want to consider the following questions:

- Is there a noticeable force between the magnets?
- How would you describe this experience?
- Does the distance or alignment affect this force?
- In what manner do you sense the existence of these forces.

Record your observations here:

Part B: Repeat the experiments outlined in **Part A,** but with the **unlike** poles of the magnets facing one another (i.e. North and South).

- Do you notice any subtle force between the **unlike** poles of the magnets?
- In what manner is the interaction between the **unlike** poles similar and/or different to the **like** poles?
- Does the distance or alignment affect this force?
- In what manner do you sense the existence of these forces

You may record your observations here:

Part C: Briskly rub the palms of your hands together for 10 seconds or so. Now hold your hands with the palms facing each other about ½ a meter or two feet apart. Slowly and gently bring your palms closer together and hold them about three cm (1/2 inch) apart for one minute. Just be curious. Pay attention to what—if anything--you are feeling in your palms or notice in the space between your hands. After a minute, begin to experiment by slowly pushing your palms closer together and then drawing them apart. Try moving them in circles in the same and opposite directions.

- Does distance matter?
- Do you sense any resistance?
- What does it feel like when you pay attention to the space between the palms of your hands?
- What happens when they are not aligned in the plane or you move your palms in circles?
- Can you see/sense any type of forces interacting between your palms?
- Did you notice any similarities between the interactions of your palms and that of the magnets?

You may record your observations here:

Part D: Place one magnet in clear plastic bag and lay it on a flat surface. Sprinkle metal clips, iron filings and/or thumbtacks over the magnet. This will be your stationary magnet. Its okay if some items clump or stick to others. Take the other magnet, your moving magnet, and put it in another plastic bag. Slowly pass it over the stationary magnet staying about 5 cm away. Repeat several times. When you have finished, hold the moving magnet over a piece of paper and take the magnet out of the bag.

- What happens when you pull the moving magnet over the stationary magnet?
- What happens to the collected debris when you take the moving magnet out of the bag?
- Are you able to do this same exercise with your palms? Why or why not?

You may record your observations and/or summarize your thoughts in the space below.

In Magnesia—an ancient city in Asia Minor--lumps of a dark shiny rock (magnetite) were found to attract bits of iron. This unusual force was named magnetism. It was soon discovered that, when suspended, one end of the magnetite always pointed north (magnetic north) indicating that magnets have two distinct poles—arbitrarily called N and S. This device became a valuable tool for navigation and evolved into the compass. When iron filings are sprinkled around a magnet, they tend to collect in a characteristic pattern indicating the magnet exerts influence beyond its physical boundaries. This region is known as a magnetic field. The magnetic field interactions of typical bar magnets are shown in **Fig.19**.

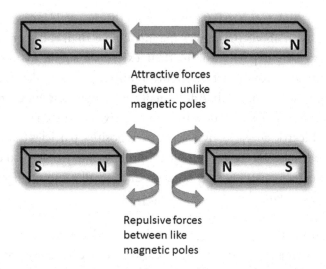

Attractive forces
Between unlike
magnetic poles

Repulsive forces
between like
magnetic poles

Fig. 19 Diagram of Magnetic Fields and their Interactions

During Part C of Activity #6 you may have noticed a squishy or bouncy feeling in the space between the palms of your hands. This same "squishiness" is noticeable when two **like** poles of bar magnets are brought together. In both cases, the sensation intensifies as you move your palms or the magnets closer together while it weakens as you move them further apart. Clearly, your hands produce a subtle magnetic field; which, like those of magnets, weakens with distance.

The elegance of the iron filings lies in their ability to reveal the unseen. Our senses tell us something is pushing or pulling but somehow "seeing" these lines of force gives them validation. Magnetic fields are produced by materials containing iron (mainly iron oxide (Fe_3O_4)) and, to a lesser extent, substances containing nickel, cobalt and a few rare earth elements. Although most materials are influenced by magnetic fields some substances such as copper, aluminum, magnesium, gases and plastics are considered non-magnetic. Tiny crystals of magnetite can be found in some bacteria as well as, the brain of bees, termites, fish, birds and humans. These crystals sense the Earth's magnetic field, and are believed to help with navigation.

The strength of a magnetic field is described in terms of **gauss**. A typical fridge magnet is 50 gauss, while the earth's surface varies from 0.3 gauss over most of S. America to 0.6 gauss around the magnetic poles. At present, more is known about the earth's magnetic field than those produced by your body. This is partly due to their extremely subtle nature e.g. the magnetic field of your heart is roughly a million times weaker (10^{-6} gauss) than the surface of the earth. Additionally, it is important not to confuse N and S magnetic poles with positive and negative electric charges. They are different. Electric charges can be isolated as positive particles (protons) and negative particles (electrons) but no matter how many times you divide or cut up a magnet you will continue to produce smaller and smaller magnets each complete with their own N and S poles.

In the early 1800's, Hans Oersted discovered electric currents could influence a compass needle. While repeating Oersted's experiments, Andre-Marie Ampère found that when electricity flows through two parallel wires in the same direction, the wires attract one another. This is exactly like the attractive forces between opposite magnetic poles. Conversely, when electricity flows through two parallel wires, in opposite directions, the wires repel one another (Fig. 16). Ampère was amazed by his results as he realized electricity could be used to create magnetic fields! Many devices including: electric motors, transformers, and metal detectors make use of Ampere's discovery. Scientists wondered if the opposite could also happen i.e. could magnets be used to create electric currents?

For 10 years, Michael Faraday strove to generate electricity, using magnets. He conducted many experiments and one in particular involved wrapping two separate coils of wire around an iron bar as illustrated in **Fig. 20**. The first coil, **A**, was connected to a battery and electricity flowed through this coil producing a magnetic field. The second coil, **B**, was not connected to a power source but was connected to a device used to measure electric current. As long as the current was running in coil **A** there was no effect. But when the circuit was switched off or on, electricity suddenly flowed through the second coil. Apparently, a changing magnetic field was needed to produce an electric current! Faraday published his results in 1834 and called this phenomenon **electromagnetic induction.** Today, this principle is widely used in many types of electrical generators.

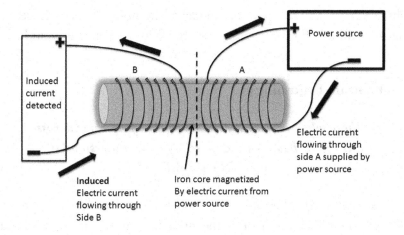

Fig. 20 Simplified Diagram of an Induction Coil

There are many animations of electromagnetic induction available from technical to basic. The following is a good place to start.

https://www.youtube.com/watch?v=gfJG4M4wi1o

So far Part 2 has explored the mysteries of electric and magnetic fields and established the following basics:

- stationary (static) electric charges produce an electric field
- moving electrons induce a magnetic field
- stationary magnets produce magnetic fields
- moving magnets induce electric currents
- light exhibits both electrical and magnetic properties i.e. it is electromagnetic

It is important to remember the universe is filled with electromagnetic energy including that produced by living things. The principles of physics remain the same whether you are working with wires and magnets in a laboratory or studying electrical and magnetic changes in the human body. The next two sections (**5.4** and **5.5**) delve into the relationships amongst light, electrons, and the quantum model of the atom. These topics set the stage for **5.6**; which investigates the energy fields generated by your heart.

5.4 Quantum Beginnings

"Those who are not shocked when they first come across quantum theory cannot possibly have understood it"
—Niels Bohr

The solar system (Rutherford-Bohr) model of the atom was presented in **4.4** as a springboard for exploring the intimate nature of electricity in your world. This included an introduction to

- atomic structure
- chemical bonding,
- formation of ions in solution
- conduction of electric charges in living organisms.

In this section, you will explore the atom at a more profound level--an important step towards understanding your own connection to light and its role in the structure and function of your heart's bio-fields. The gift of this upheaval is it demands an entirely new perception of reality--a perception that is beginning to percolate into humanity's pulse.

Have you ever wondered how astronomers can identify which elements are in the stars? Or how a crime scene lab can identify a chemical in a speck of dirt. The key is in the light! Years of research shows, that each element emits a unique pattern of light. In fact, this pattern is so precise it is called the *fingerprint* of the atom. By comparing the frequencies of light emitted (and/or absorbed) by a substance, it is possible to identify the elements it contains. The sun for example is composed of hydrogen and helium while the remote star TT Cyngi is made of carbon and oxygen. Analysis of light produced by matter is called **spectroscopy**. It embraces the entire range of the electromagnetic spectrum and is widely used in many areas of science.

A partnership between light and matter was an idea that rocked the scientific world. Glimmers of this relationship began in 1887 during Hertz's study of radio waves. At one point, he shone ultraviolet light on the electrodes in his spark gap apparatus (5.1). As he did so, Hertz was astonished to find the voltage changed. Other research followed and it was soon recognized that when any material-- solid, liquid, or gas-- absorbs light it enables electrons to escape. This escape of electrons leaves the material with a positive charge and is called the **photoelectric effect.** Planck's formula, the photoelectric effect and spectroscopy, were all major contributors towards Bohr's confirmation of the integral relationship between light and matter.

The following link has excellent visuals summarizing Planck's work, spectroscopy, and the photoelectric effect.

https://www.youtube.com/watch?v=_2fcDqr39Jk

The question now becomes what is the connection between light and physical matter? Light is intangible and elusive while matter is just the opposite-- concrete and obvious. A deeper understanding of the atom is integral to illuminating this concept--excuse the pun! Remember the solar system model of the atom from **4.4**? In that section, the electrons were simply described as being organized into energy levels located outside the nucleus of the atom. How did scientists arrive at this conclusion and why was this important?

It began when Planck's formula (**E = h x f**) revealed the quantum nature of light. (**5.2**). In a stroke of genius, a Danish physicist by the name of Neils Bohr decided to explore the possible connections between Planck's equation and the "fingerprint" of each element as revealed by spectroscopy. He proposed that the energy released (and absorbed) by electrons was quantized. With this in mind, he undertook a meticulous study of the bright line spectrum of hydrogen--the simplest atom. Using Planck's formula, he was able to calculate the differences in energy between each band of visible light as seen in hydrogen's spectrum. His work led to a brilliant insight—in atoms, the energy of an electron packaged. The year was 1913.

Later it became evident that the energy of each electron determines its location. Those closest to the nucleus, or in the first energy level, have the least amount of energy. To move further away, an electron needs to gain a specific amount or quantum of energy. Just like light, each quantum is a whole there are no quarter or one-half energy levels. Conversely, when an electron loses energy, it goes down one or more energy levels and releases a quantum of light corresponding to the energy released. This means the fingerprint, or bright line spectrum of each atom, as used in spectroscopy, is determined by specific quanta of energy held by its electrons. This can be summarized as follows:

1. each electron possesses specific amounts of energy or quantum
2. a quantum of light is absorbed as the electron jumps from a lower energy level to a higher one
3. a quantum of light is released when the electron jumps from a higher energy level to a lower level.

Although inaccurate by modern standards, the Rutherford-Bohr model provided a useful steppingstone as it eroded the popular, mechanistic view of the universe and paved the way for the quantum atom. As more, and more discoveries emerged it became increasingly apparent a new perception of the universe was needed. The West began to look at the philosophies of the East to help understand the seemingly inexplicable experimental results of scientists. The evolution of the modern quantum atom had begun.

5.5 Quantum Basics

"The task is not to see what has never been seen before, but to think what has never been thought before about what you see everyday."
—Erwin Schrodinger

The study of traditions such as Taoism and Buddhism opened doorways to innovative views of matter and the universe. Unlike the west, these approaches were holistic and integrated. They provided desperately needed scaffolding and insights to help explain what research exposed. Physicists such as Fritjof Capra and Michael Talbot allude to the shockwaves these discoveries sent through the scientific community. Waves so potent that many bodies of wisdom have yet to assimilate the profound nature of a quantum universe. This section will highlight the incredible contributions of three physicists: Heisenberg, deBroglie, and Schrodinger who forever changed humanity's perception of reality.

When I was younger, I often had trouble deciding. Sometimes there seemed to be so many factors to consider, the more I thought about it, the more difficult it became to make the *right* choice—especially when choosing from a box of chocolates! I recall being told on several occasions "not to decide is to decide" which made things even more confusing. Nature is fuzzy too, there is a limit to what can and cannot be known regarding the behavior of subatomic particles. Even atoms it would seem can be uncertain as Werner Heisenberg discovered.

In 1927, Heisenberg found he could not measure the exact position of a particle and its momentum at the same time and vice versa. i.e. if you measured the particle's position, you could not be certain about its momentum. Like a teeter-totter, the more precisely one of these values is known, the less precisely the other can be determined--regardless of the one that is measured. Heisenberg had discovered an element of uncertainty in the universe. He summarized his findings by stating any change in the position of a particle times any change in its momentum is greater than or equal to a constant. This can be written as:

$$\Delta \text{ x } \Delta \text{ p} \geq \textbf{a constant}$$

Δ= change in, **x** = position, **p** = momentum

N.B. The constant is usually Planck's constant (**h**) divided by 2π

Now known as the **Uncertainty Principle**, it negates the idea of pure objectivity. In fact, research has confirmed the very act of observing interferes with what is observed i.e., an individual's energy, experiences and beliefs contribute to and are not separate from the outcome(s) whether they are conscious of this or not. How is that for connectivity? The following video provides a good visual explanation of The Uncertainty Principle.

https://www.britannica.com/science/uncertainty-principle

Now that nothing is ever certain thanks to Heisenberg, let's return to the study of light and see how deBroglie gave birth to the mindboggling topic of **dualism**. The controversy around the nature of light was described in section **5.1**. Fans of Huygens' work favored the wave model--especially after Young's double slit experiments. On the other hand, advocates of Newton's theory, believed light was made of particles. Light it seemed had a dual nature sometimes it behaved like a wave and other times like a particle. So what was it?

Further advances in research strengthened the case for the duality of light, it also sent scientists into a tailspin. How could light be both? Enter, Louis deBroglie and the **wavicle**! In 1924, he submitted his PhD thesis on the dual nature of matter. Initially, it appeared so radical that it was almost refused yet ironically, this same paper was awarded the Nobel Prize for physics only five years later. In his paper, deBroglie proposes that all matter has both a wave and a particle nature. Size, however, matters so the smaller the particle, the more important its wavelength and vice versa. Very tiny particles such as a photon have a significant wave nature but for massive objects such as the Earth its momentum is more important. The equation is written as:

$$\lambda = h/p$$

λ = wavelength, **h**= Planck's constant, **p**= momentum,

N.B. momentum (**p**) is the same as mass x velocity (m x v)

The PBS's series <u>Space Time</u> has excellent footage explaining the double-slit experiment and the implications which led to deBroglie's equation. Here's the title and link:

<u>The Quantum Experiment that Broke Reality | Space Time | PBS Digital Studios https://www.youtube.com/watch?v=p-MNSLsjjdo</u>

By 1926, scientists had the following pieces of the puzzle for the quantum atom:

- Planck's quantum nature of light
- Bohr's quantization of electrons in atoms
- Heisenberg's Uncertainty Principle
- DeBroglie's wavicle

The burning question was how any of these ideas might be connected let alone contributed to an eloquent understanding regarding the structure of matter? The clues to this puzzle begin with the sea and a beautiful lagoon called Manson's Landing on Cortes Island BC. At low tide, on a warm summer's day it offers acres of fascinating marine life to explore. As the tide turns, the sea abruptly surges back through the narrow entrance forming large waves and strong currents that rapidly fill the lagoon. My family has delightful memories of riding these waves and "flying" in on them as they rush to refill the lagoon. The fierceness of this change poses very real hazards for small children and non-swimmers; which is where tide tables come in handy!

The power and speed of tidal changes has always been a concern for those on and around the ocean. The influence of the moon and sun upon the tides had been known for eons, but a more precise tool for predicting tides was needed. In 1867, Sir William Thomson developed the mathematics of waves which led to the prediction of tides and the tide tables.

While searching for a cohesive explanation of the atom, Erwin Schrodinger was inspired to apply Thomson's wave equations to the spectrum of the hydrogen atom. They fit elegantly and the modern quantum atom was born. To this day, it continues to challenge everything scientists thought they knew about the universe.

Let's take a brief look at the basics of the quantum model. First of all, although electrons still exist in energy levels they do not travel in rings. Instead, the electron exists as a *matter-wave* and its energy determines the likelihood of its location within a cloud of possibilities. Imagine walking into a steam room. The swirling steam makes it difficult to see as the clouds of steam continuously move about you. Just as you cannot pinpoint the exact location of the steam, the same holds true for an electron. The visible steam resembles the most likely location of the electron (90% chance) and is known as an electron cloud or **probability distribution.**

Although the electron is most likely to be within the cloud--just like the steam in the room—it may leave and could be found anywhere--even infinitely far away. **Fig. 21** shows a spherical cloud. It is most likely the electron in a hydrogen atom would be found in this region of space. The clouds become more complex in larger atoms as they acquire more electrons and the density of each cloud decreases as you move further away from the nucleus. In each case, the electrons are probably within their designated cloud but due to its uncertainty it is not a guarantee!.

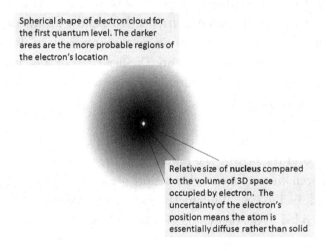

Spherical shape of electron cloud for the first quantum level. The darker areas are the more probable regions of the electron's location

Relative size of **nucleus** compared to the volume of 3D space occupied by electron. The uncertainty of the electron's position means the atom is essentially diffuse rather than solid

Fig. 21 Diagram of a Spherical Electron Cloud

Frequently, I have been asked how energy can go through solid objects like wood or the human body. This too has to do with your perspective. Imagine yourself on a miniature spacecraft the size of an electron. As you navigate thru atomic space it would be like flying through our solar system in terms of all the empty space. Just a your imaginary spacecraft has much room to maneuver inside the atom energy also has room to penetrate and interact with the particles which make up the atom. Consequently, you could never "land" on the surface of an atom because there is no solid boundary where the atom begins or ends.

When you touch or look at a solid in the normal world, the atoms are just more closely packed than in a liquid or gas. Your senses can't detect the huge regions of space occupied by the electron clouds around each and every nucleus. Metaphors such as "solid as a rock" or "I am a rock" further ingrain the idea of the impenetrable permanence we associate with solid matter. So much so that it is a very tough naïve conception to change. Yet at the atomic level, the exterior of all atoms—even those who make up your body--are just dense associations of electrons. When enough energy is applied to vaporize a solid to a liquid and then to a gas, there is plenty of space amongst the atoms for objects to pass through. If you are tiny enough, like the size of an electron, it is easy to move amongst the atoms of a solid so in a sense, it is all relative!

Larger atoms have more electrons and more complex arrangements of their electron clouds. It is the three dimensional arrangements of the electron clouds that are partially responsible for the type of chemical bonds that will form and the resulting shape of the new substance. From a molecule of water to DNA, to a human being, the possibilities are amazing! The following animation link gives a good introduction and summary of electron clouds, energy levels and the quantum atom in general.

https://www.youtube.com/watch?v=Q9Sl1PYSyOw

As scientists continue to delve into the structure of the universe more and more intriguing discoveries are being made. It is now widely accepted that electrons, protons and neutrons are composed of even smaller particles called quirks and quarks that seem to have an energy ecology all of their own. Although fascinating, it is for another book in another time. For now it is important to remember the modern quantum atom is:

- the basic unit of physical matter
- a microcosm of integrated quanta of energy
- a mathematical model
- largely empty space

You now have the basic tools for **5.6**; which looks at what is meant by an electromagnetic field, especially that of your heart.

5.6 Your Heart's Field

"The coherent energy patterns of the heart center during moments of love apparently has the ability to influence energetic events in the body, as well as the potential to influence distant events"
—**Richard Gerber**

On a hot summer's day, I love being able to plunge into the ocean near my home. The cold water is always shocking—it makes me gasp, skyrockets my heart rate and covers me with goose bumps. I swim fiercely at first, until I warm-up. No matter how mentally prepared I think I am, my body reacts instantly and globally to the cold water. Humans are born reactive and possess a number of healthy reflexes including rooting, startle, and grasping. All are deemed essential to survival and used as part of the learning process is to distinguish between what is and is not a real danger. As discussed in **3.3** your SNS behaves like a distant early warning system and even as you mature, it can act instantly before any conscious awareness of the danger exists. Where does it get such information?

Research has found that those who have been abused and/or are suffering from PTSD (**post traumatic stress disorder**) may startle more easily and have a greater chance of being triggered into "fight or flight" mode than others. This condition is known as hyper vigilance. Many athletes, soldiers and first responders hone their ability to access an acute state of global awareness. Interesting new evidence indicates such super fast signaling is faster than what the human nervous system can actually process. More importantly it suggests this communication occurs via energy fields. This section, introduces the basics of energy fields and their emerging role in biological systems and particularly that of your heart.

When you hit a baseball, push a wheelbarrow, or pull a wagon, you are using a force that directly touches and affects another physical object. This type of force is known as a **contact force**. Other forces such as gravity, magnetism and electricity act through a distance i.e. they do not need to be in direct contact with an individual or object to exert their effect. Recall from Activity #6 that you can sense magnetic attraction and/or repulsion before the poles of the magnets touch. Indeed the magnetic forces seem to surround and permeate the area near the magnet. The region of space through which this type of a force may act is known as its field. Previous discussions of electricity and magnetism focused on the how these discoveries affected the laws of physics. How might they relate to biology?

Historically, ancient Egyptian, Chinese, and Greek traditions have used magnetite for healing. In 1773, Franz Anton Mesmer revived this use of magnets for healing his patients and frequently noticed unusual currents moving through their bodies. Mesmer discovered that he could sense a sort of attraction and repulsion around the client similar to the sensations he had when working with magnets. Even more interesting, he found he could produce the same effect by using his hands above the body of the patient. In what manner are magnetic fields related to the human hand?

To properly address this question, its necessary to revisit what is known about electric and magnetic fields. When Franklin (**4.4**) rubbed glass with fur, he built up a stationary electric charge and generated an electric field. Similarly, a fixed magnet produces a magnetic field. As long as there was no movement of charge, these two seemingly different fields can be formed. However, when Faraday (**5.4**) pioneered electromagnetic induction, it became apparent that even the tiniest movement of a charge, instantly created a field with electrical and magnetic components--an **electromagnetic field** (**EMF**). Maxwell's (**5.1**) equations and the development of the quantum atom (**5.6**) consolidated the inseparable, quantum nature of both electricity and magnetism.

Glimmers of how this might relate to humans began with Einthoven's groundbreaking work on the heart's electrical activity as discussed in **4.8**. The cascade of change accelerated during the 1930's with Harold Burr's curiosity about electricity in living organisms (**4.3**). His detection of minute electric signals showed that life is formed and/or controlled by tiny electric and magnetic fields. Around 1935, he proposed the integration of these micro-fields was responsible for the generation of a much larger electromagnetic field radiating from your body, the **Human Energy Field (HEF)** or aura.

Like many, Burr was ahead of his time and his research was not well received until the latter part of the 20th century. By then, significant advances in quantum physics and technology had provided irrefutable evidence that every event in your body, normal and pathological, produces changes in your HEF. Consequently, scientists went from total disdain regarding the existence of a human energy field to absolute conviction that it did exist.

Before delving further into the human energy field, it is important to examine a few of the unique properties of an electromagnetic field. The EMF is described as a physical field extending infinitely throughout space. Charged objects produce the EMF. This means that you and everything else in the universe is always immersed in the EMF. Most humans are oblivious to its existence, as the sense organs are not trained to perceive this incredibly subtle field and its fluctuations.

Electromagnetic interaction is considered one of the four fundamental forces of nature (the others are gravitation, weak interaction and strong interaction). Not only does it cause charges and currents to move, these charges and currents also affect the field. The EMF is dynamic and interactive. Once a field has been produced, charged objects in its vicinity will experience a force from this field but in return, they will also affect the field. A concert is a simple metaphor for this exchange. As the musicians begin to play, the venue fills with music and engages the audience. The engagement of the audience (clapping, dancing, singing along etc.) reinforces and enhances the performance of the musicians. This results in greater audience engagement and so on. Despite their different roles, there is constant interaction and change. Similarly, every action you make sends ripples of interactions outwards through the electromagnetic field like ripples in a pond.

In **5.1**, the electromagnetic spectrum was discussed so where then does light fit into the EMF? When an EMF is far away from the charges and currents of its origins, it no longer has much of an effect on the field even though it continues to propagate. When this happens, it is known as light or **electromagnetic radiation** (**EMR**) and includes the entire range from radio waves to gamma rays. Consequently, you are largely unaware of the ocean of EMR and EMF in which you are immersed your entire life.

Another exclusive property of the EMF is that it is packaged or quantized just like light. This concept does not make sense in day-to-day life and is generally misunderstood. Most people believe fields behave like charged particles and this is absolutely not the case! Electrons move slowly through matter at a fraction of a centimeter (or inch) per second while EMF fields propagate at the speed of light i.e. 300 thousand kilometers (186 thousand miles) per second. Quantized fields are a million times faster than charged particles and in the quantum world things happen instantly!

What does this have to do with your heart? For many years, I have collected research to help link what I know as a scientist with what I experience as an energy practitioner. Energy work requires the activation of the palm chakras; which includes entering a state of heart-centered compassion. Clients would say they could feel "heat" from my hands even if I wasn't touching them. Often my hands felt as if they were burning. I believed the energy emanating from my hands was real but how was this happening and why did it work?

One day, when I was still teaching school, I asked a colleague if he knew of any devices that could detect really subtle energy. He told me to look into the SQUID magnetometer. SQUID stands for Superconducting Quantum Interference Device and it is designed to detect very weak magnetic fields. This machine was important and finally, I began to get some answers!

The role of electricity in living things has been researched since Galvani's time (**4.3**) and its therapeutic use may be a few thousand years old. By the early 20th century, biologists knew that the tissues and organs of the human body generated electrical fields. However, despite the fact quantum physics deemed electricity and magnetism inseparable; magnetic fields in the body were unknown. Biologists assumed they either did not exist or were not important to life.

This assumption fell apart in 1973 when researchers at Syracuse University in New York found a magnetic field projected by a human heart. Shortly thereafter, scientists at MIT, using the SQUID, validated the existence of the heart's magnetic field. Later, they discovered smaller magnetic fields emanating from the brain. This was exciting stuff and eventually led to the realization that all the tissues and organs in the human body produced signature magnetic (or **bio-magnetic**) fields. Each of these fields have a doughnut like shape and are known as a **torus. Fig. 22.** Illustrates the torus generated by your heart. It is now known that each of these fields coexist within the larger torus shaped field of your body. Such discoveries were eloquent validations of Burr's predictions and effectively married quantum science and biology.

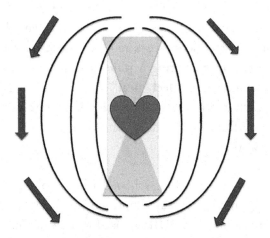

Arrows show direction of continuous energy flow from the top, throughout the field and back into the bottom of the torus

Fig. 22 Diagram showing the Energy Flow in a Torus

Burr's research on the HEF produced other gems. For example, the beginnings of a disease could be detected in the human energy field before physical symptoms appeared. He believed that if somehow, the normal balance of the HEF could be restored, the progress of a disease could be reversed. Burr's prediction was correct. SQUID instruments have now been used to map changes in bio-magnetic fields caused by various stages of illness or trauma. Other tools that have been designed for such diagnostic mapping include:

- Magnetic Resonance Imaging (MRI) creates pictures of the human body using magnetic fields, radio waves and electric field gradients.
- Magnetocardiograms (MCG) measure the magnetic field of the heart
- Magnetoencephalograms (MEG) record the magnetic field of the brain

Let's return to Mesmer's discovery about human hands and magnets. In the early 1980's at the Colorado School of Medicine, Dr. John Zimmerman studied the effect of hands on energy treatments with a SQUID magnetometer. He found a large bio-magnetic field emanating from the palms of the practitioners. Seto et al (1992), duplicated his work and included practitioners of QiGong, Yoga, Therapeutic Touch, and other energy practices in his study. He recorded magnetic pulsations from the practitioner's hands that averaged between 7 and 8 Hz—the same as the earth's magnetic field. Equally astonishing, these signals were synchronized with the brain frequencies of the practitioners as they swept through a range of 0.3 to 30 Hz. The field strength emanating from their palms (10^{-2} gauss) was 1000 times stronger than the electromagnetic field of the human heart (10^{-6} gauss) and one million times stronger than the field produced by the brain (10^{-8} gauss).

As a stand alone, this work may seem to border on the fringes of magic or illusion. However, it is now possible to "jump start" the healing process using **Pulsed Electromagnetic Field (PEMF) Therapy.** Research has demonstrated that specific frequencies can stimulate the growth and repair of many different tissues e.g. bone, nerves, skin, ligaments and so on. Successful repair of injuries-- even 40 years old--have been facilitated in this manner. As a medical device, the PEMF induces minute electrical currents to flow in nearby tissues and is based on the same physics of electromagnetic induction discovered by Faraday almost 200 years ago.

Even more exciting was the discovery that the optimal frequencies needed for healing these tissues are in the same range as those emanating from the hands of energy therapists. Energy therapists have a distinct advantage in that they can vary the frequency of their magnetic pulses. This enables them to address a variety of injuries involving different tissues in one session rather than using several PEMF devices for a few weeks. Additionally, scientists have found living tissues to have the same electronic circuitry as the SQUID. This means humans have "built-in" magnetic field detectors and helps explain why energy practitioners can detect the distorted energy fields of damaged or diseased tissue with their hands.

So far we have established that your heart is an electrical and magnetic organ. The electrolytic solution of ions that bathes all of your tissues and organs is responsible for transmitting the electrical signals that stimulate your heartbeat. These same ions conduct electrical signals from your heart and other organs throughout your entire body. Cumulatively, this profusion of electrical signals contribute to the creation of your heart's electromagnetic fields and those of your other organs and tissues.

More importantly, your heart produces the largest amount of electrical and magnetic energy in your body. In fact, it is some forty to sixty times stronger, than the second biggest source, your brain. The beating of your heart creates its own bio-fields and they too are in the shape of a torus as shown in **Fig. 22.** Additional and ongoing research has shown that bio-fields of your heart interact with and are affected by your HEF, other organ bio-fields, the HEF of others and universal energy fields. As of yet there are is still much speculation as to how these fields are organized, store and transmit information some of which appears to be faster than the speed of light i.e. quantum. What is often relegated to intuition may actually be an example of quantum information transfer. One area of interest involves the longitudinal oscillations of ions in biological systems. These arrays of ions exhibit quantum behavior and may offer a mechanism for the sensitivity of humans and other living organisms to quantum fields.

How often do you know if someone is behind you before see him? Do you ever get an intuition of an event or something about to happen before it does? Emanations from your heart's bio-field can be detected as much as 15 or more feet away from you and actually spread to infinity. Furthermore, studies reported by the HeartMath Institute found that in every instance, the heart reacted to a stimulus before the brain. This means the heart "knows" an event will take place before your brain. Your heart's field could be part of your distant early warning system and/or intuition. It may be that listening to your heart is more important than you think.

A good documentary of how quantum physics and biology intersect by physicist Jim Al-Khalilli titled: The Secrets of Quantum Physics—Quantum Biology Theory Documentary

https://www.youtube.com/watch?v=gT22gRzyotA

James L. Oschmann, PhD has links to a variety of excellent, leading edge videos, books and research on many aspects of the science behind energy medicine. His website can be found at http://www.energyresearch.us

If you are interested in more technical research on the physics of bio-fields and quantum biology, Glen Rein PhD has amazing work on his website as well. Please visit

http://www.innobioteck.com/home.html

While Part 2 explored the fusion of quantum physics and the electromagnetic field of your heart; Part 3 is designed to uncover the secrets of your emotional heart and the pivotal role it plays in shaping all of your life experiences--despite your thoughts on the matter!

PART 3

YOUR EMOTIONAL HEART

"What's love got to do, got to do with it
What's love but a second hand emotion
What's love got to do, got to do with it
Who needs a heart when a heart can be broken"
—**Graham Hamilton Lyle & Terry Britten**

Overview

Part 2 began with a look at electricity and its role in the nature of your physical existence. This culminated with the recognition of bio-fields--most notably those of your heart--and their subtle yet, integral, contribution to the web of life. Many frequencies of light are embedded in these fields; which work synergistically to create your physical body. Living organisms are beings of light but how do bio-fields interact to fashion the spectrum of your emotional experiences. In what manner is your heart braided with body, mind and spirit?

As a small child, I have distinct memories of witnessing my maternal grandparents engaged in horrendous arguments. On such occasions, our mother would scoop up my baby sister and we would rush out the door to head home. I didn't understand what was going on but I knew it made me afraid of the people I loved. A few years later, my grandmother started having frequent asthma attacks and it became normal for us to dash to their house and help her with the oxygen equipment or if severe, call the ambulance. I recall asking my mother why this was happening and she said, "All the fighting is making Grandma sick". Although this was my first exposure to the idea of illness resulting from emotions and thoughts (**psychosomatic**) the memories remain vivid.

According to Caroline Myss, our "biography becomes our biology" as emotional forces influence the physical tissues within our bodies. Some of the early discoveries linking emotions, heart and biochemistry lent insight as to how emotions affect health. Ranging from romantic love to bone chilling fear, Part 3 builds upon the previous chapters and explores the complex interplay amongst your heart, health, and emotions.

CHAPTER 6

YOUR HORMONAL HEART

6.1 Love is all you need?

> *"All you need is love*
> *All you need is love*
> *All you need is love, love*
> *Love is all you need"*
> **—The Beatles**

During my teens, I would dance around to this and other love songs, dreaming of the perfect romantic relationship. Like most young people, I believed in the *happily ever after* life idealized in Cinderella type stories. Then one day you are *love* struck. When it happens, your heart is so full it feels like it will burst and everything is and will always be amazing! What more could you need? Oh, but no one ever tells you there is a difference between love and lust. Nor how your hormones and emotions can lie to your heart, let alone the heartache of a broken love affair.

Years later, when I taught human reproduction, I often began with a short True and False questionnaire about love and romance. I found this helped put the biology of sex into a more relevant context and the ensuing discussions were always an eye opener. Expectations—mostly unrealistic--about a future partner were hotly debated and often remain an issue well into adulthood. At some point in the class, the topic of *love at first sight* always emerged which was my cue to introduce the Sweaty T-shirt experiments.

Just as you have a unique heartbeat, and fingerprint, you also have your own *odorprint*. The Sweaty T-shirt experiments were designed to see if personal scent had an effect on sexual attraction in humans. Co-ed groups were divided into female and male cohorts. Each participant wore a clean T-shirt during a sweaty workout. Afterwards, their sweaty T-shirts were coded and put into sealed bags while DNA samples were obtained from each participant. Next, the females were instructed to smell each of the T-shirts submitted by the males and rate them from most to least attractive. The same procedure was repeated but this time, the males smelt the females' sweaty T-shirts. Neither set of participants knew the identity of the sweaty T-shirt's owners.

The results were surprising. Using smell alone, the females differed in their choices of the *most attractive* male. The same held true when the males rated the females. In both cases, each participant chose T-shirts belonging to individuals whose DNA was the most different from their own. So when you are instantly attracted to that special person across a crowded room, it may be called love at first sight but research suggests that *lust* at first scent was the real trigger. This is nature's way of choosing a partner with the greatest differences in DNA to ensure the maximum in genetic diversity of any children produced. Unfortunately, it does not mean you are well suited in terms of personality, beliefs, or interests etc., they are more likely to fall under the category of luck.

The video "Sweaty T-Shirts and Human Mate Choice" provides an entertaining overview of this research.

https://www.youtube.com/watch?v=WcovKsjvVgM

The chemicals responsible for the control of behavior in humans and other animals thru scent are called **pheromones**. Such messages are common and may range from ants laying down chemical trails to the powerful aphrodisiacs secreted by silk moths--detectable for several kilometers. Not only does chemistry work behind the scenes in the choice of your mate, it controls you from birth and well before that. Hormones, behave as the traffic control monitors of your biochemistry. They have nudged you and your parents this way and that well before your birth to make you lovable, to help you grow and thrive. For what could be more worthy of love than new life?

Newborn babies embody your blissful beginnings. They represent the blossoming of life filled with the amazing potential to give and receive love, joy and peace. It is your inheritance. As you navigate the roller coaster of life things get complicated. Some experiences plunge you into heartaches of anger or fear while others can be uplifting, even exciting. Regardless, every event, and every experience leaves subtle chemical and energetic impressions in your cells and tissues. Over time, these lingering impressions shift the delicate balance of your physiology in a myriad of ways and can disconnect you from your heart. Activity #7 provides an opportunity for self-exploration of your emotional heart before more amazing connections amongst hormones, and your heart are revealed.

EXPLORING LOVE

Time: 20 min.

Objective: To reflect upon, your personal experiences, thoughts and ideas about love in order to move deeper into a personal awareness regarding the role of love in your relationships to self and others.

This activity can be completed in a variety of ways. Choose whatever manner feels right for you. Suggestions include, writing your answers in this book or a journal, recording your thoughts, or simply meditating on the questions. The questions are roughly organized into a timeline representing the stages of your life and you are encouraged to elaborate upon what else was going on in your life during each phase. The questions are not restricted to the stages either. If one or more appeals to you in a different stage feel free to muse about it wherever it holds the most personal relevance. When you reach the end of your present timeline you may choose to speculate on how you might feel or would like to feel as you approach future stages in your life.

Stage A: Early childhood (0 to 5 years)

Did you feel loved by your family as a small child?

What did it feel like?

Stage B: Childhood (6 to 11 years)

As you grew, did you still feel loved in the same manner as in your early years? Explain

At this stage of your life were you able to feel and express love for others? Why or why not?

Stage C: Teen years (12 to 18)

How did your feelings of love about yourself and others change as you entered adolescence?

What was it like to have or not have a young love?

What made your heart sing?

Stage D: Young adulthood (19 to 29)

What if any changes in your ideas of love took place during this time?

How do you know if you are loved or not?

What makes your heart ache?

Stage E: Adulthood

Are you able to give and receive love easily or is this difficult? Explain your answer

Can you look at yourself in the mirror and honestly say, "I love who I am"? Why or why not?

What is your heart's passion?

Additional Space for your Reflections:

Activity #7 used a broad brush to jog your memory and get you thinking about the different ways in which love was or was not experienced in your life. It also sets the stage for the upcoming sections wherein the profound relationship between your emotions, and their biochemical regulation, are considered. Becoming aware of the complex nature of love and the many roles it plays from birth to adulthood is an important facet of your own inner work. Moreover, how you give and receive love is intimately braided within the chemistry of your heart and its bio-fields.

6.2 Bonding and You

"There is no instinct like that of the heart."
—Byron

To this day, the most incredible experiences in my life were the birth of each of my sons. Glimmers of their existence began with vague flutters, like a tiny fish, swimming in my belly. Over time, these movements became more intense, even painful towards the end as they kicked and squirmed inside me. Previously, I'd felt in control of my body but as new life grew inside of me I became a bystander--the vessel so to speak. During university, I was fortunate enough to observe the amazing development of fertilized eggs in the embryology lab, but my studies had not provided an instruction manual on how to make a heart, design a limb, or grow a new human being. It just sort of happens and is an immensely humbling experience. Although much remains a mystery, it is now understood that a cascade of chemical reactions regulates growth and development from embryo to adulthood and scent plays a potent role in this process as well. Babies know their mother's scent and mother's savor the almost intoxicating odor of their newborn. This is linked to and reinforces a new mother's desire to hold and nurse her baby.

Breast-feeding is also elegantly linked to a hormone called **oxytocin**--the milk "let-down" hormone. Discovered by Sir Henry Dale in 1905, oxytocin was found in extracts from the pituitary gland and plays a vital role in the development of bonding between mother and child. The maternal act of touching and holding a newborn releases oxytocin in the infant and serves to calm and soothe the baby. Simultaneously, the act of holding the newborn stimulates the release of oxytocin in the mother and brings her deep comfort as well.

The release of oxytocin is not limited to infants. Gentle, soothing touch, such a hand on a shoulder or a kind hug stimulates the release of oxytocin in teens and adults of all ages. For this reason, it has been dubbed the *cuddle hormone* and plays a pivotal role in the development and maintenance of all positive relationships amongst humans. This applies to both genders and includes family, friends, lovers, colleagues and pets. In fact, numerous studies by psychologists such as Harry Harlow in the 1950's and Rutter et al in 2007 have shown the detrimental effects on infants and children who are not held or touched in a comforting manner. To this end, many hospitals are embracing programs wherein volunteers spend time holding premature and/or ill babies on a daily basis.

Adults too need this type of interaction and the introduction of pet visitations in seniors' homes and prisons have been very successful for similar reasons. Sadly, many people from all walks of life have not been touched with gentle intentions for a very long time. The importance of a simple kind touch reinforces the efficacy of complementary therapies that use touch as part of their protocol such as Massage Therapy, Healing Touch or Reiki. Along the same thread, when my children were small their favorite song was "Ten Hugs a Day" by Charlotte Diamond. Evidently, it carried an important message to families because recent studies have confirmed getting five hugs a day for four weeks increases happiness!

The release of oxytocin lowers the reactivity of a part of the brain called the amygdala. Consisting of two almond-shaped clusters located deep within the temporal lobes of the brain, they are responsible for integrating emotions, emotional behavior, processing memory and motivation. The global effects of oxytocin start at birth however it is produced throughout your life and contributes to the healthy maintenance of many important aspects of your physiology and emotional health. The benefits of oxytocin are summarized as follows:

- Reduces fear and anxiety
- Acts as an antidepressant
- Decreases agents responsible for inflammation (e.g. **cytokines**) and thus speeds up wound healing
- Promotes romantic attraction and monogamous pair bonding
- Increases generosity and empathy
- Increases uterine contractions for birth and delivery by stimulating the release of prostaglandins
- Promotes positive social interactions and pro social behavior such as trust and attachment between individuals
- Inhibits the development of tolerance to addictive drugs (opiates) and reduces withdrawal symptoms
- Inhibits the release of stress hormones (adrenocorticotropic hormone and cortisol) by calming the sympathetic nervous system
- Lowers blood pressure and increases secretion of urine

In essence, your biochemistry was finely tuned from birth--with the help of oxytocin--to establish a powerful attachment between you and your caregivers. This is just the beginning of what nature intended as a partnership of unconditional love. This programing is so strong that it can make mothers into superheroes if their child is in danger like lifting cars off their children with one hand while preparing dinner with the other--just kidding! Incredibly, recent studies have found that your heart also produces oxytocin! This has vast implications especially since the role of cell receptors in opiate addictions was discovered—the topic of **6.3.** More exciting news is forthcoming including further discussion and an illustration of oxytocin in **6.4.**

6.3 Opiates and You

"...the molecules of our emotions share intimate connections with, and are indeed inseparable from our physiology. It is the emotions, I have come to see that link mind and body."
—Candace Pert

This story begins with the poppy. Valued for its naturally occurring opiates (morphine and codeine), it was cultivated in Mesopotamia as early as 3400 BCE. Throughout history, many battles both global and personal were, and continue to be, waged over this flower. The search for even more potent painkillers led Alder Wright to develop a synthetic version of morphine. The year was 1864 and his new drug was one and a half times more potent. It was named **heroin**. Heroin's popularity for pain relief soared because of its ability to induce a rush of bliss and euphoria The Bayer Company (of aspirin fame) actually sold heroin as an active ingredient in their cough medicine from 1898 to 1910 until the extreme nature of its addictive properties became apparent. By then heroin's damage to human life had already begun.

Nonetheless, chemists continued to search for other potent derivatives of opium and soon developed hydromorphone and oxycodone. During the 1960's and 70's, further experimentation led to the synthesis of fentanyl and carfentanyl, which are respectfully 50-100 and 10,000-100,000 times more powerful than morphine. The unprecedented toll these opiates have on addicts, and those who accidently touch the dust (e.g. first responders) has led to a surge in the demand for drug overdose kits. Enter **naloxone** (brand name **narcan**), a crucial antidote to opioids. Patented in 1961, it blocks the action of opioids but the how and why of opiate addiction was unknown.

As biologists learned more about the outer boundary (**cell membrane**) of a cell, some of the answers to opiate addiction, the action of hormones, and the regulation of life in general began to surface. In the beginning the cell membrane was seen as a simple border with gateways separating the inside of the cell from the outside--like a flexible house with different doors

113

and windows. Today, it is seen as a dynamic, intelligent guardian fully capable of interacting and responding to other cells and the environment in a myriad of ways. Cell membranes control what enters and leaves each and every cell in your body and much of this traffic is regulated through specialized molecules (**receptors**); which are embedded in the membrane.

Receptors behave like designer locks wherein each receptor receives and bonds exclusively with particular messengers. As this occurs, an energy exchange takes place that briefly changes the structure of the cell membrane and opens the "lock". This subtle structural and energetic shift stimulates a cascade of biochemical reactions unique to the receptor involved. A multitude of biological processes are regulated in this manner ranging from the manufacture of proteins to the release of neurotransmitters (**4.7**). In this manner, ongoing communication and collaboration amongst the cells, and tissues of your body is maintained. As it turns out, the key to understanding opiate addiction was also linked to the knowledge about receptors.

In the early 1970's, Hans Kosterlitz tested known opioids on the intestine of a pig. Each slowed the activity of the gut tissue--causing constipation. He was able to identify opiate receptors in the intestine and suggested that their ability to relieve pain was probably linked to the presence of opiate receptors in the brain. At that time, any notion of your body sending messages to alter the behavior of your brain was considered absurd. Consequently, his work was largely dis-regarded, as many of his contemporaries did not believe such a receptor could possibly exist. They assumed your brain's role was to receive, interpret and act upon information. Like the conductor in an orchestra, the brain was believed to send chemical messages (neurotransmitters) such as norepinephrine and dopamine (**2.4**) to control your body in a top down or one-way system of communication.

In *Molecules of Emotion*, Candace Pert describes her research with great wit and brilliant insights. As a young doctoral student, she was convinced that receptors for opiates existed in the brain but after many failed experiments she was stuck. Then she realized that some substances might bind with a specific receptor for longer periods than others. Following this line of thought, she predicted that morphine, and its relatives, might bond to their receptors for a short time. While the antidote naloxone on the other hand, must bond for a longer time period. This meant that naloxone essentially blocked the receptor for morphine and other opioids. Her hunch was correct and she successfully demonstrated the existence of opiate receptors in the brain. Her discovery was extraordinary because scientists were finally able to demonstrate that:

- a chemical basis for your emotions existed.
- changes in your biochemistry can cause changes your brain.
- changes in your thoughts and feelings can produce changes your body.
- all humans (and animals) possess the same opiate receptors for creating bliss

Pert's work verified that brain and body were both players on the same dynamic and interactive team and opened a floodgate of discoveries including the role of **peptides** in coordinating the entire team. Although the brain might seem like the captain it accomplishes very little without engaging the entire team. Even more exciting was emerging evidence that your heart is the all-star when it comes to peptide production and is a strong contender for the position of team captain.

6.4 Peptides and You

"It is one of the more striking generalizations of biochemistry—which surprisingly is hardly ever mentioned in the biochemical textbooks—that the twenty amino acids and the four bases, are, with minor reservations the same throughout Nature."
—Francis Crick

All living things --from bacteria to humans—are made from proteins. The study of peptides and their importance began in the early 1800's with the discovery of proteins. As most athletes know, proteins are important for building strong muscles, but that is not all they do! They are integral to life and your entire anatomy and physiology depends on proteins in one form or another. The vital roles of proteins include:

- formation of the tiny structural networks known as **microtubules**
- storage and transmission of information through sophisticated codes such as DNA.
- function as enzymes which catalyze all of your biochemistry
- function as hormones,
- coordinate movement,
- provide structural support,
- control immunity,
- regulate growth and reproduction and more!

Obviously, proteins are fundamental to life and are critical component of a healthy diet. Infants and children have the supreme need for proteins in order to support normal growth and development. In countries where the overall supply of food is limited they have the highest risk of developing a syndrome known as **kwashiorkor**. The lack of protein in their diet impairs their intestinal function to the point that their frail bodies cannot make the enzymes needed to digest what little food they do receive. This leads to reduced immunity and poor liver function; which does irreducible damage to the delicate physiology of the child and is partially responsible for the high rate of infant mortality in destitute countries.

Just as matter is made from the elements, proteins are made from building blocks called **amino acids**. The first amino acid was discovered in 1820 by Braconnot and was named **glycine**. During the next century or so, others were discovered to make a total of twenty common amino acids, plus a few others that are somewhat rare. Your body is able to make eleven of them from a variety of sources including carbohydrates. These are considered the non-essential amino acids and consist of:

- alanine, arginine asparagine, aspartic acid, cysteine, glutamic acid, glutamine, glycine, proline, serine, and tyrosine.

The remaining nine must be part of your diet and are deemed essential. All of them can be found in meat, fish, eggs, and dairy products. Plants sources however, must be consumed in specific combinations such as grains and legumes e.g. beans and rice, in order to obtain the full complement. Essential amino acids include:

- threonine, valine, tryptophan, methionine, histidine, isoleucine, phenylalanine, lysine, and leucine.

All amino acids are identified by the presence of two specific groups of atoms. One is called the **carboxyl** group (-COOH) and the other an **amino** (-NH$_2$) group. When the carboxyl group of one amino acid joins with the amino group of another a **peptide bond** is the result. **Fig. 23** illustrates peptide bond formation.

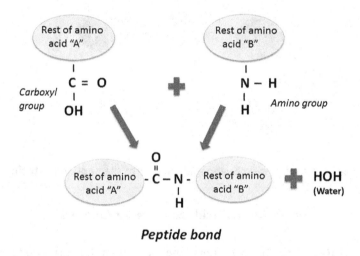

Peptide bond

Fig. 23 Diagram showing the formation of a Peptide Bond

The peptide bond is extremely strong. Initially it could only be broken down by boiling the protein in strong acid, anywhere from a few hours to several days (this is also why your stomach produces hydrochloric acid). This process was so time consuming that by 1975, only thirty peptides had been assigned specific chemical formulae.

Construction of a protein begins with the selection and sequencing of the necessary building blocks. Anywhere from two to hundreds of amino acids are used to make a chain. Just like letters in the alphabet are used to make words, each amino acid can be sequenced in a multitude of ways to make thousands of different chains. Shorter chains--two to one hundred amino acids-- are called **peptides** while longer ones are labeled **polypeptides**. Many structural proteins such as microtubules are made from several polypeptide chains that are twisted, folded, and/or woven to form a 3D shape described as its **conformation**. This process is like creating a sculpture from strings of beads.

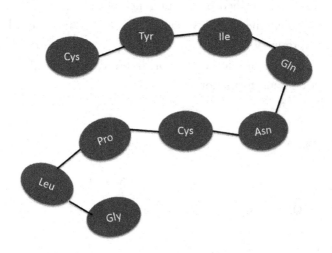

The sequence of nine amino acids that form the peptide **oxytocin**

Fig. 24 Amino Acid sequence for Oxytocin

Oxytocin (**6.1**)—the bonding hormone--was the first peptide to be made in the laboratory and sometimes, it is hard to believe this small chain of 9 amino acids is responsible for so many aspects of how you interact with the world. The significance of oxytocin has recently become even more profound as oxytocin inhalers are now being used to support the treatment of post-traumatic stress disorder (PTSD) and autism. Additionally, exciting research by Paigi et al (2016) has found that the use of OT inhalers increased compassion towards woman in both the control and PTSD groups. The sequence of amino acids for oxytocin is shown in **Fig. 24**.

The study of peptides and their importance continues to expand on an almost daily basis. Upcoming sections **6.5** and **6.6** consider the impact of two relatively new, but very important groups of peptides—endorphins and heart –both of which have enormous effects upon your emotional wellbeing.

6.5 Endorphins and You

"I just realized that I can't heal physically until I can heal emotionally and that part of me feels so disconnected"
—**Anonymous**

Initially, research on the study of pain and pain management gave birth to many of the discoveries about peptides. For example, when you injure yourself, it is a natural reaction to hold the wounded area. Often this happens before you are even aware of the act. Previously, this behavior was considered a simple reflex until experiments showed that a person's experience of pain is lower when they, or someone nearby holds the injured area. The perception of pain is even lower still if you hold the hand of someone who loves you. In fact, a study from Stanford University School of Medicine found passionate feelings of love provide pain relief that is just as effective as opioids.

Dr. Jean Watson's studies on Caring Sciences or **Caritas**, dovetail eloquently with these discoveries. Her research demonstrated a patient's perception of whether or not their nurse(s) cared about them was significantly linked to their rate of recovery and experience of pain. The more they felt cared for, the faster their recovery and the lower their pain levels. The ability of oxytocin to reduce inflammation and to lower the stress response was presented in **6.1**. What other peptides might be released when people receive a collage of heart centered caring, and gentle touch? The answer lies in your body's ability to produce its own opioids called **endorphins.**

Prior to your birth, it was natural for you to squirm and kick in the womb—sometimes it may have even been a bit too much for your mother's ribs! From conception to death, movement is as essential to your health as breathing. Babies and children are programmed to move as a critical part of their growth and development. Exercise makes you feel better and contributes to your overall health and wellness way beyond the obvious building of strength and stamina. So much so that improved circulation and elevated heart rate alone do not explain the significant mood altering states e.g. the runner's high, induced by exercise. Scientists agreed that the body must produce a natural opioid but what was it, and where was it produced?

Less than three years after the discovery of the brain's opiate receptors, a Scottish team of investigators found the body's natural opioids. They were eventually called endorphins (aka enkephalins) and the name was derived from two words, endogenous (meaning produced within the body) and morphine. Later, in 1975, this same team identified the five-peptide sequence for two forms of endorphin i.e.

- Tyr-Gly-Gly-Phe-Met and
- Tyr-Gly-Gly-Phe-Leu.

Endorphins are your own form of morphine and regardless of whether you are experiencing a state of bliss from exercise, sexual orgasm, or meditation, etc., the receptors are the same. Initially, endorphin receptors were believed to be limited to the brain, especially in areas associated with emotional control like the **limbic** system. Recent studies have shown endorphin receptors occur in many key areas of the body and are not limited to the brain as previously thought. Cells from the intestine, immune system, nervous system and heart have all been found to possess endorphin receptors. It now seems that these receptors form an amazing, integrated information network throughout the body. More than twenty endorphins have been identified and some such as beta-endorphins are stronger than morphine. The body's release of endorphins is triggered by a variety of factors including:

- ultraviolet light,
- exercise,
- laughter, watching or reading comedies, telling jokes
- hot chili peppers,
- moderate intake of alcohol,

- stress,
- sex,
- meditation
- bodywork (massage, Healing Touch, Reiki etc.,)
- chocolate
- long term loving relationships
- music
- aroma of lavender or vanilla

Many conditions ranging from alcoholism and obesity to aging of the brain have been linked to low levels of endorphins and/or receptors. Endorphins are involved with your heart's interactions and the control of your autonomic nervous system in order to contribute to a healthy relaxation response Although much is yet to be learned about these molecules they play a crucial role in the regulation of your heart and emotions.

But wait, there is more—according to Barron (1999) not only does your heart have endorphin receptors it produces endorphins! Further research on the ability of the heart to produce opiates will provide insights into how feelings of love and gratitude can induce euphoria even when someone is experiencing pain or trauma. Your heart's ability to release opioids and its impact on health and wellness has tremendous implications for your relationships with self and others.

6.6 Your Heart Peptides

"Too often we underestimate the power of a touch, a smile, a kind word, a listening ear, and an honest compliment, or the smallest act of caring, all of which have the potential to turn a life around."
—Leo Buscaglia

Mastery of your emotions requires understanding and acceptance of their pivotal roles in your existence and learning how to work constructively with your individual biochemistry. Unfortunately, when people are in emotional turmoil all too often, they resort to either suppression of their emotions or unmitigated demonstrations of emotions. As we shall see, neither of these choices is good for your heart, or you, and both impair the ability of your heart to function at it's very best. In this section you will look at some more astonishing basics about the chemistry of your heart—they might even cause your heart to skip a beat or too!

Investigations carried out between 1971 and 1983 revealed information about your heart's ability to produce hormones. The implications of this work were vast. So much so that an entirely new field of study called **psychoendoneuroimmunology (PENI)** evolved. This work strives to integrate developments in the fields of psychology, endocrinology, neurology and immunology in a holistic manner. Such groundbreaking work has forever changed our understanding of your emotional heart and many now believe your heart is more important than your brain with respect to regulating your health and emotions. These discoveries and more are the theme of this section.

In the early 1960's, the electron microscope was used to study the muscle cells of your heart. It was noted that the cells of the atria were different than these of the ventricles. In fact, they appeared to have more in common with the cells producing hormones in your endocrine system. The important features common to both atrial and endocrine cells include:

- abundant systems for manufacturing cell products (**rough endoplasmic reticulum**)
- highly developed structures for packaging and storing cell products (**golgi apparatus**)
- storage granules specific to the cells of the atria

The reason for these differences remained a mystery for almost two decades until de Bold and his colleagues tested rats with extracts from heart atria. They were excited when they found these extracts had three very significant effects:

- decreased blood pressure (**vasorelaxation**),
- increased need to urinate (**diuresis**),
- increased amount of sodium ions excreted in the urine (**natriuresis**).

The combination of these factors reduces the total volume of blood in your circulatory system. This in turn decreases the workload on your heart and slows the heart rate. Astonished, they realized the heart's atria was secreting a hormone capable of controlling a totally different area of your body--in this case the kidneys and urinary system. Its' identity remained a mystery for three years until it was unveiled in 1984. It was named **atrial natriuretic peptide (ANP)** and a new revolution in the understanding of your heart had begun.

Soon, other exciting research demonstrated your heart and aorta both produce oxytocin (OT). Even more astonishing was the discovery that the release of oxytocin stimulates the release of ANP (Gutkowska et al). These findings have a profound impact. They signify that the release of OT acts to slow the heart rate and lower blood pressure by stimulating the release of ANP as follows:

- caring or gentle touch releases oxytocin
- oxytocin induces the release of ANP
- ANP slows the heart rate and lowers blood pressure
- the body shifts into the parasympathetic state i.e. relaxation is induced

This cascade of biochemistry is an excellent example of how kindness and gentle touch have an immediate effect not only on your heart, but the entire body. No wonder crying babies need to be held and people who are sad, or ill feel better when someone holds them. This poignancy of such discoveries also supports the efficacy of complementary therapies such as Healing Touch Program®.

Shortly after the discovery of ANP, another polypeptide was found in your heart. This time it was located in the ventricles and was labeled **brain natriuretic peptide (BNP)** although the heart is the main source. BNP is secreted when there is increased pressure or stretching of the ventricles and it mirrors the effects of ANP as listed previously. Normally BNP blood levels are lower than ANP except in the instance of heart failure (and other life threatening events) in which case, it increases as much as 100 times.

Blood levels of BNP consequently, make a good diagnostic tool for certain types of heart disease.

As more of this story evolved, other peptides produced by your heart e.g. **cardiac natriuretic peptide (CNP)** were discovered. All are crucial for maintaining your health e.g. Vesely et al (2007) found as much as two-thirds of breast cancer cells in mice could be eliminated using four of the cardiac peptides. That's not all, growing evidence has established the use of cardiac hormones for heart attacks, congestive heart failure, kidney disease, and to support the immune system. Not only is your heart at the core of emotional health; it is the source of a new family of information molecules whose potential for healing has only just begun.

CHAPTER 7

YOUR COHERENT HEART

7.1 What is heart coherence?

> *"If you look underneath your depression, you'll find anger. Look under your anger, and you'll find sadness. And under sadness is the root of it all, what's really masquerading all the while—fear."*
> **—Carolyn Stearns**

The importance of **heart coherence** and **heart rate variability (HRV)** are introduced in this chapter. This includes a discussion of the factors that affect heart coherence, such as trauma and addictions. Suggestions as to how you may heal your emotional heart develop greater coherence and listen to the wisdom of your heart complete this chapter.

As a young girl I was fascinated by knitting and loved to watch the strands of wool flow through my mother's hands as she rhythmically created a garment. As soon as I could hold the needles I begged her to teach me how to knit. It's not as easy as it looks and although my first blankets were full of holes, I don't think my dolls minded! Patience and practice are needed to produce smooth, regular stitches. Although each stitch is individual, they are all formed from the same continuous string and every stitch is connected to all the other stitches. If you pull on one stitch, all the neighboring stitches shorten up to compensate and if you cut the yarn in any spot, the entire piece may unravel.

The smooth regular stitches formed by experienced knitters are parallel to the ECG patterns of coherent heartbeats. Just as the height and frequency of stitches will vary with the size of the knitting needles, so will the height and frequency of the peaks in your ECG vary with your activity levels. This is known as heart rate variability. If you are working hard e.g. climbing stairs the peaks will be higher and closer together. If you are resting, the peaks will be lower and further apart. Regardless of your activity level, a healthy heartbeat shows a smooth and coherent pattern just like a well-knit garment. On the other hand, if you are experiencing stress, trauma, anxiety etc., then the peaks and valleys in your ECG will be jagged and irregular like the ill-formed stitches of a beginning knitter. Such patterns in your ECG are described as incoherent. **Fig. 25** illustrates the differences between a coherent and an incoherent heartbeat.

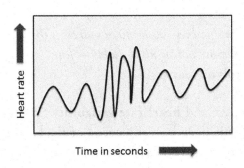

Fig. 25-A Simplified diagram of an ECG showing the smoother, rhythmic curves of a coherent heartbeat regardless of heart rate. These patterns are also associated with positive emotions such as gratitude, love, and compassion.

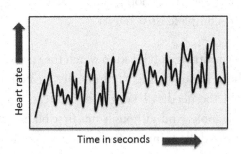

Fig.25-B. Simplified diagram of an ECG showing the erratic, spikey patterns of an incoherent heartbeat regardless of heart rate These patterns are associated with negative emotions such as anger, frustration and stress.

**Fig. 25 Generalized Diagram comparing
Coherent and Incoherent Heartbeats**

Although regular exercise is known to improve emotional health in many ways including the release of endorphins (**6.2**), your physical fitness does not have a direct relationship to heart coherence. Basic fitness is determined by how quickly your heart responds to and recovers from physical exertion. If you are fit, your heart rate will increase rapidly to adjust to a workload and return to its normal rate faster than someone who is less fit. However, even the very fit may have incoherent heart rhythms and vice versa and the longer you endure a negative emotional state, the more incoherent your heartbeat becomes. In some cases, this can be linked to adverse experiences, as far back as early childhood. Along the same line, Ginsberg et al (2010) studied the HRV of returning soldiers and found both heart coherence and HRV was lower in those soldiers diagnosed with PTSD compared to the those that did not have such a diagnosis.

For many, an incoherent heartbeat can be so ingrained that it feels normal. This aligns with developmental research; which indicates children who grow up in a chaotic home often create drama and chaos in their current relationships or environment to achieve their perception of normalcy. To such individuals what is disturbing and dysfunctional to others is actually familiar, and oddly comforting to them. On occasion, I have had clients make statements alluding to this viewpoint e.g. "if people never fight, they are not really communicating" or "I am worthless (or useless) so I deserved to be neglected (raped, beaten etc.)".

Additionally, such declarations offer insights into how belief systems can be manipulated by one's environment and provide partial explanations why family members may condone and/or turn a blind eye to the abuse and/or trauma of other family members. Although all abuse is unacceptable, the invisible scars from emotional and mental abuse are often more destructive than the physical ones. In some families, dysfunctional patterns of abuse can be passed on from generation to generation and become so ingrained that it meets with very little resistance and/or no one believes the victim-- even when they get up the courage to tell someone. Incest and sexual abuse of young children appears to be particularly prone to this pattern.

An ECG therefore, not only records the electrical activity of your heart, it serves as a window into the history of your emotional world. The relative coherence, or lack thereof, in an ECG provides insights into experiences, both negative and positive. Along this line, the HeartMath Institute has developed personal technology for monitoring heart coherence. These tools help improve an individual's ability to cope as they learn to self-regulate their emotional triggers. However, before true heart healing of pain and fear can be realized, there are fundamental issues at the core of your being that must be addressed on a deeper level. Discussion of these issues and more are braided throughout the following chapters of this book.

7.2 Heart Breaks and You

"The patients that I worked with—I'm talking about hardcore, street level drug users, people injecting cocaine and heroin and so on—not a single one of them ever came to me and said, "Doc, I was traumatized, and I'm using that as an excuse to do drugs." They didn't know they were traumatized. No doctor had ever pointed it out to them. They thought they were just fuck-ups. They thought they were just bad people. They thought they were just addicts. They didn't realize that they were using the addiction to soothe a deep pain that was rooted in trauma. In all cases of addiction that I have seen, there's deep pain that comes out of trauma. The addiction is the person's unconscious attempt to escape from the pain".
—Gabor Mate

As a child, I have many memories of being woken up during the night to find the lights on and my wonderful mother cleaning or cooking because she couldn't sleep. At the time, I just thought mom was acting a bit weird and went back to sleep. At some vague point in time, I noticed that she didn't get up in the night as much. I remember her telling me she was taking sleeping pills, but it was okay as lots of her friends, even some who were nurses, were taking them. This began during the sixties, when sleeping pills were quite strong and freely prescribed. They were also highly addictive which was not well known at the time.

Over the years, mom shared stories about her childhood terrors. Night after night in an effort to escape the violence of their parent's arguments, she and her sister hid in the closet, or under their beds. Both had nightmares most of their adult lives, displayed obsessive-compulsive behaviors and suffered from anxiety and depression. Even in her nineties, my mother would fight panic attacks if she thought they might forget her sleeping pill. She was compassionate, optimistic, funny, intelligent and loved by many. Very few however, even suspected the invisible demons she strove so hard to overcome her entire life.

The word *trauma* has become more commonly used in everyday conversations. Challenging life events used to be described as *upsetting* or *disappointing* and some topics such as abuse were simply taboo. Today, extreme expressions such as *devastated* or *traumatized* are common and people seem more stressed than ever. To a certain extent, this openness has backfired and instead of galvanizing greater support for one another, it seems to have overwhelmed many and dulled their empathy for others--especially those who have been deeply traumatized. The question as to whether life is any more difficult today than it was 50 or 500 years ago is a moot point. Nevertheless, there is an eternal nature to basic human needs and the need to love and be loved is primal.

Compassionate support of those who have endured trauma is pivotal with respect to breaking these patterns of addiction. Addictions come in many forms, some more obvious than others and include drugs, alcohol, pornography, tobacco, food, sex and violence. Moreover, the victims of trauma are not the only ones who suffer as it translates into dysfunctional relationships with family, coworkers and friends. In some cases, it is passed on from one generation to the next.

Although the research on PTSD still has many gaps, one emerging piece that holds great significance is related to traumatic experiences as a child. The study of **Adverse Childhood Experiences (ACE)** has revealed individuals who endured trauma in their younger years have less resilience. Recent studies have shown trauma can activate survival-oriented behaviors that lead to addictions. As a result, ACE children are at a much greater risk for developing PTSD and/or addictive behaviors as they encounter challenges later on in life. This type of research contributes towards an understanding as to why two people who endure a traumatic event e.g. the same car accident, can have very different reactions to the incident i.e. one will develop PTSD while the other does not. Furthermore, most ACE experiences are never diagnosed, let alone acknowledged, so they frequently lurk below the surface or remain as hidden emotional time bombs.

While experiencing a trauma doesn't guarantee a person will develop an addiction, research indicates trauma is an underlying source of addictive behavior. According to Dr. Dan Bilsker (2011), men commit 80% of the suicides in Canada, and currently it is peaking at age 55. When asked how they handle emotional distress, men say, "I'll drink more". The following statistics are from a report issued by the *National Center for Post-Traumatic Stress Disorder* in the United States:

1. 25 to 75 percent of people who survive abuse and/or violent trauma develop issues related to alcohol abuse.
2. 10 to 33 percent of survivors from accidents, illness or natural disasters report alcohol abuse.
3. diagnosis of PTSD increases the risk of developing alcohol abuse.
4. female trauma survivors who do not struggle with PTSD face increased risk for an alcohol use disorder.
5. male and female sexual abuse survivors experience a higher rate of alcohol and drug use disorders compared to those who have not survived such abuse.

People are important. Everyone needs to feel they matter and are worthy as human beings. To this end, much has been written regarding the significance of creating a comfortable, safe environment in homes, classrooms, workplaces and other social settings. It is especially important in all types of medical and complementary therapies. This must be augmented by the therapeutic presence of someone who truly listens, is empathic and nonjudgmental whether it is a parent, teacher, supervisor or therapist.

In my private practice, I have frequently been humbled by the experiences clients reveal when I've asked them simple, neutral questions such as, "What would you like me to know about you?" or "What else was going on in your life when that happened?" For many, it may be the first time anyone has ever asked them that sort of question. When they feel safe enough to share their pain and fear, it seems to galvanize the release of their heart's burden. Equally important, is seeing someone write down what they choose to share as this gives their words validity and confirms that they have been heard. This type of engagement provides an opportunity to gain clarity and reflect upon what has happened without the drama. This is often a crucial first step for putting trauma to rest. Activity #8 follows and is intended to help you reflect upon some of the experiences in your life that you would like to heal.

ACTIVITY #8

EXPLORING YOUR
PAIN AND FEAR

Time: 20 min.

Objective: To reflect upon those experiences or situations which trigger pain and/or fear in your life in order to bring them forward for releasing and healing.

This activity can be done in any manner that feels best for you. You may want to address one question at a time over a period of weeks or simply do the entire set of questions quickly and then come back to them at another time. Journaling or drawing your answers is a very helpful way to establish a record for yourself and meditating on the questions is also a useful strategy. When recalling traumatic events do not become engaged in the drama. Watch it like it is a TV show, as if from a distance, just be a curious observer. This exercise is not intended to have you "relive" trauma.

(Please note this activity is not intended as professional help. If you need or are under psychiatric care please consult your physician before completing this exercise.)

1. What is it you would like others to know about you but are afraid or ashamed to tell them?
2. Where do you hurt the most? Do you remember when it started and what was happening at the time?

3. What do you truly fear? What do you feel was the root cause of these experiences?
4. What are your triggers? When did they start and how would it feel if they no longer controlled you?
5. What strategies have you found useful when you need help coping with your life?

Additional thoughts or reflections about this activity:

Activity #8 was an invitation to delve into some of the sources of those components in your life that may cause fear, pain, sadness anger etc. Although these experiences are part of life, they do not have to control you forever. Neither are they simple to release. The next section looks at emotions from a deeper level and is intended to provide insights into healing your emotional heart.

7.3 Mending Your Broken Heart

"Doing something positive will help turn your mood around. When you smile, your body relaxes. When you experience human touch and interaction, it eases tension in your body."
—Simone Elkeles

Can you die from a broken heart? Probably not but sometimes your heart can hurt so much it feels like you might. There is a medical condition called *broken heart syndrome* or **takotsubo cardiomyopathy**. Characterized by a weakening of the left ventricle in the heart, it is brought on by severe emotional or physical stress such as domestic violence, severe pain, or the unexpected loss, illness, or injury of a loved one. The main symptoms are chest pain and shortness of breath; which mimics a heart attack. Although most cases of broken heart syndrome resolve within several weeks as the person recovers from the stress, medical attention should always be sought. This section explores the effects of both negative and positive emotions on stress and their ability to help mend a broken heart.

During any emergency, your body's instant, global response is to flood the bloodstream with epinephrine. As it moves into high alert, survival is the focus and fear becomes the dominant emotion. Fear is intertwined with a pounding heart, shaking knees, sweating, and high levels of epinephrine. In one experiment, subjects were given epinephrine before watching a horror movie. They showed more negative facial expressions, more intense fear, and more negative memories of the film than the control subjects. The same degree of emotional enhancement e.g. more amusement with an amusement film etc., has not been observed with other emotions.

Epinephrine it seems plays a very powerful role in the encoding of those memories, and emotions generated by fear. Fear is the body's primal and primary response to stress before you are even conscious of it. Regardless of whether the stress is real or imagined, it magnifies fear and opens the gateway for this emotion. Once unleashed, it can be overwhelming and often leads to a cascade of other negative emotions such as anger, hate, jealousy, pain, rage, anxiety, grief etc.

Candace Pert once proposed that if peptides and other information molecules are the biochemical triggers of emotions, then the body is the unconscious mind. Repressed trauma caused by overwhelming emotion is stored in the body part affecting the ability to feel or move that part of the body. This has certainly been my experience both as a practitioner and as a patient.

As a practitioner there have been numerous occasions where I have been working on diffusing what seemed like a heavy or congested area of the client's physical body and/or energy fields. Later, during their debriefing, the client has shared that when I worked on this area they remembered a forgotten accident or trauma and felt it soften and release as I worked

134

on the area. I too have experienced such releases especially after I was in two car accidents less than four weeks apart. They were both serious and the injuries were roughly the same in each case. I had significant mobility issues, and it seemed as if the repeated trauma solidified my injuries. During energy treatments, I too experienced releases in specific areas similar to what my clients had expressed when receiving a session.

Such experiences are further supported by new research indicating specific and unique physical responses by the body to each emotion. Nummenmaa et al (2013) compiled a bodily map of human emotions using over 700 subjects from both Caucasian and Asian backgrounds. Their study revealed each emotional state is associated with sensations in topographically distinct areas of the body. *Happiness* for example results in a global activation of the entire body especially in the head and chest. *Fear,* on the other hand, shuts down the arms, legs and lower abdomen. Some activity remains in the upper torso, but it is significantly less than that observed for happiness. Questions such as "where does it hurt" or "where do you feel this" can now provide even greater insights into emotional experiences. This discovery also supports further integration of allopathic and complementary therapies, as it would appear humans really do have *issues in their tissues.*

Activity #8 provided an opportunity to survey your negative emotions and their underlying sources. This too is vital with respect to healing your emotional heart. In 1996, Daniel Coleman wrote *Emotional IQ.* At the time, it was well known that those who were the happiest and most successful in life were not necessarily those with the highest IQ's. Motivated by this and other factors, his book reveals that the manner in which you manage emotions, whether they are your own or somebody else's determines your emotional intelligence. There are five main aspects:

1. Recognizing your own emotions
2. Managing your own emotions
3. Self-Motivation
4. Recognizing other's emotions
5. Managing relationships

Take a few minutes to rate yourself from poor to excellent for each of theses five aspects. You may want to use the space provided below or your journal to reflect upon the items you assigned lower scores to and/or consider how you might improve in these areas:

For most, recognizing emotions are one thing but managing them is another. This is especially true for those emotions connected to fear due its powerful relationship to epinephrine as described earlier. According to Gabor Mate, delving into the source of your emotions is a crucial piece:

> *"What interests me is for people to really know where they are coming from and where their actions come from. People can act the right way, but that doesn't mean they are being the right way. You can't force emotions; you really have to know what they are. For me, the important question is, what are the actual emotions underneath the actions that are driving my behavior and where do those emotions come from? For me, it's not a question of acting into the right emotion. It's a question of understanding what are the source emotions from which we are acting….if we actually understood that all behaviors are for the most part coping mechanisms for emotions that we are not able to deal with, then the focus could shift not just to changing behaviors, but actually understanding the emotions that underlie them. That's what I think is missing from medical practice. Whether it's addictions or whatever it is, we are not seeing what's driving it and what's underneath it."*

Based on these ideas, it makes sense to combat stress and fear by consciously engaging in behaviors that are known to reduce epinephrine levels and its effects upon the body, emotions and mind. In **2.1**, stress and its ability to alter the dance between the sympathetic and parasympathetic nervous systems was described. This was followed by discussion of some of the strategies known to have a positive influence by stimulating the PNS. Strategies such as exercise (**2.2**), breath work (**3.1**), relaxation techniques (**3.2**), and happiness (**3.3**) and their effectiveness at moderating stress were discussed in some detail. You may wish to revisit some of these sections and experiment further now that you have a deeper understanding of your underlying triggers.

Currently, **vagal tone**; which refers to the activity of the vagus nerve has become a noteworthy topic with respect to managing emotions. The location of the vagus nerve was described in Activity 2 (Step 1, Part 6) and it is the 10th cranial nerve originating from the medulla oblongata in the brainstem. It travels down the sides of your neck, across the chest and down through the abdomen. Its activity can be measured using an ECG and is a reflection of your heart rate variability as discussed in 7.1. Some people have stronger vagus nerve activity than others which means their bodies can relax faster after stress. Studies on twins have shown that there is a genetic component to vagal tone and some are born with a naturally higher tone than others. Lifestyle is also a factor as poor vagal tone is associated with those who don't exercise. A strong vagal response is associated with better regulation of blood glucose, and reduced likelihood of diabetes, stroke and cardiovascular disease. These people are also socially and psychologically stronger, better able to concentrate and remember things. They tend to be happier, and more empathetic.

On the other hand, those who have low vagal tone are often plagued by autoimmune disorders including irritable bowel syndrome, asthma, diabetes, chronic fatigue, pain and obesity. They are more likely to suffer from depression, inability to focus, social isolation and a lack of empathy. In 2010, Barbara Fredrickson and Bethany Kok studied the relationship between vagal tone and wellbeing. Vagal tone was measured at the beginning of the experiment and nine weeks later at the end. Half of the participants were taught a meditation technique to promote feelings of goodwill towards themselves and others. At the end of the study they found a significant rise in the vagal tone and a greater increases in positive emotions amongst the group that meditated. This was the first research to demonstrate that increased positive emotions and goodwill towards others can improve vagal tone.

In the same vein, Sue Hitzmann, creator of the MELT Method®--also known as myofascial energetic length technique--has developed techniques and tools to help regulate and balance the ANS and improve heart rate variability. She recommends the following for restoring vagal tone:

1. Cold showers
2. Sing, laugh, and hug
3. Alter heart rate variability
4. Reduce jaw tension
5. Decompress your neck
6. Stimulate lymph flow in hands and feet

Even more exciting are recent studies on the impact of positive emotions and health. Kim et al (2016) completed a long-term study on aging by US Veterans. The results showed that overall psychological distress (measured by anxiety) compared to wellbeing (measured by happiness and life satisfaction) had opposite effects on the DNA activity related to heart disease. In other words, those who had high levels of anxiety produced higher levels of the gene activity responsible for inflammation of the heart and its arteries. Opposite results occurred, for those subjects with high scores for happiness and life satisfaction; which most certainly supports previous discussions on the role of happiness in reducing stress.

Living in the moment has become a popular phrase for very good reason. Many people get stuck on the emotional drama around the tragedies and stories of their past and/or fears of their future--often unconsciously. As such, it keeps them in a negative loop that can actually alter their physiology as shown through the earlier example of epinephrine and the ANS; which is but one of many networks in your physiology. Until time travel is perfected, it is unrealistic to change the past no matter how much you want to. The good news is you can take the lesson(s) forward and use your experiences to make choices that are best for you at this moment in time.

7.4 Listening to Your Heart's Wisdom

"Synchronicities occur when inner knowing
and external events come together."
—Carl Jung

Have you ever had that uncanny sense or feeling that someone was behind you only to turn around and realize someone is actually there? Or have you had a hunch about something, before it happens, and ignore it only to find out later your hunch was spot on? Now there is research that not only validates these hunches but, indicates you really should be listening to those hints!

Recall from **5.6** that your heart produces the largest electromagnetic field in the body--some forty to sixty times greater than your brain. Not only does this field permeate your entire body and aura, it acts as a type of distant early warning system. Scientific evidence to support these phenomena was documented in 2004 by McCraty et al. During the experiment, individuals were placed in rooms created specifically to eliminate any outside stimulus. The volunteers were hooked up to electronics designed to measure their heart rate (ECG), brain waves (EEG) and the electrical conductivity of their skin. In this manner, the physiological responses of the heart, brain and ANS to an emotionally arousing stimulus could be recorded. In every case, the data revealed that the heart responded to the stimulus before the brain by as much as 6 to 7 seconds. This means your heart and ANS are able to perceive and respond to a stimulus before you are even consciously aware of its existence. How cool is that?

Intuition is defined as the ability to understand or know something immediately based on your feelings rather than facts. Frequently, there is no clear evidence one way or the other and you have to base your judgment on intuition. Other researchers, inspired by McCraty's research, used these same physiological measures to determine whether they could be used to detect intuitive perception amongst successful entrepreneurs and their business decisions. Their results were parallel to those of McCraty and showed information was received by the ANS some 6 to 7 seconds before the outcome of the investment choice was known. Although further research needs to be done, it seems as if following your intuition pays off in the financial world as well.

In her book *Journey to the Heart,* Melody Beattie states that the purpose of the journey is to open up and listen to your inner guidance as your heart leads you to someplace new. When your heart is filled with love for self and for others you are able to trust and surrender to something more with grace and dignity. However, this is not an easy piece in a world that is dominated by facts, the intellect and logical reasoning. It requires patience, finding time to be in solitude and following those first, loving thoughts that come into your mind without rationalizing or dismissing them as your mind tries to over-ride your intuition.

Based on the preceding discussions in this and previous chapters it is not difficult to make the conceptual leap that your heart's field is faster at perceiving the world around you, partially because of its larger size. When the idea of the field's quantum nature is brought into the equation the probability of your heart field connecting and interacting with the heart fields of others both near and distant becomes viable.

Part 3 was intended to demonstrate that you are a product of our emotions whether they are expressed or suppressed. All of your emotions affect your heart and your emotions have the power to change your DNA. By tuning into the wisdom of your heart, you can more fully access the universal energy fields in which you are fully immersed. This leads us into Part 4 wherein the interplay between your thoughts and your heart will be considered.

PART 4

YOUR MINDFUL HEART

Everyone should consider his body as a priceless gift from
One whom he loves above all,
a marvelous work of art, of indescribable beauty, and mystery,
beyond human conception, and so delicate that
a word, a breath, a look, nay, a
thought may injure it."
—Nikola Tesla

Overview

When I am teaching the ideas of synergy and holism in my classes, I bring out a toy, racing car. I then ask the students to identify the most important part of the car and explain why they think it is the most important piece. The engine or the driver, are the most common choices. Then I take the car apart and scatter the wheels, chassis, engine, driver etc., in front of the group. When I repeat my question, there is usually silence as they realize the wheels and the chassis are just as vital to the functioning of the car as the driver or the engine. Without all the pieces working together, the car is basically useless, as anyone who has ever experienced a flat tire or dead battery will tell you.

Along the same line, many fitness posters would have you believe your body is a machine. A recent one displayed a well-defined male torso beneath a bold quote by Leo Tolstoy stating, "Our body is a machine for living. It is organized for that is its nature." Although it is meant to inspire a fitness regime, there is also a subtle message implying each part is separate from the other e.g. the chest (pectoral) muscles are independent from the shoulder (deltoid). Yet, it's very tricky to move your shoulder without moving parts of your chest and, vice versa. Such declarations subtly reinforce the idea that humans are assembled like a 3-D jigsaw puzzle and the brain, like the driver in the take apart racing car, is the only important piece.

Your brain is an incredible organ. Volumes have been discovered and written about the brain and nervous system; much beyond the scope of this book. The focus for Part 4 is to survey some of the newer research revolving around the brain, and its interactions with your heart. Chapter 8 begins with the interplay between your thoughts and biochemistry. The discussion then moves on to the patterns of electrical activity in the brain and how they overlap with the heart. The importance of forgiveness, gratitude and epigenetics with respect to mind, and heart complete Part 4.

CHAPTER 8

FUSING YOUR
HEART AND MIND

8.1 How do you Perceive Your Heart?

*"Since Pavlov and his pupils have succeeded in causing the secretion
of saliva in the dog by means of optic and acoustic signals, it no
longer seems strange to us that what the philosopher terms an
'idea' is a process which can cause chemical changes in the body."*
—Jacques Loeb

The above quote refers to experiments conducted by Ivan Pavlov during the
1890's. His work led to the development of classical conditioning wherein
the control of behavior was managed thru the use of an external stimulus.
This approach was very appealing partly because one simply had to train
(condition) the desired behavior to a stimulus and eventually the stimulus
triggered the new behavior. An understanding of what going on inside the
subject was considered unnecessary. Later, research by other psychologists
such as B.F. Skinner led to systems of changing behavior through reward
and punishment as the new field of **behaviorism** evolved. Many of its
principles became popular with parents, educators and clinicians.

Even today, punishment is still the most common form of social control although research has shown repeatedly it remains the least effective way of changing behavior. Short-term punishment does not make you internally compliant, nor change your thoughts and beliefs. For example, I was an escape artist as a toddler. I recall many forms of punishment from scolding and time out, to spanking; none of which changed my behavior. In fact, I quite distinctly recall plotting my next route out of the backyard—the rose trellis-- while I was still being punished for my most recent escape. Interestingly enough my children were also quite ingenious at getting out of the backyard!

Every action from brushing your teeth to complex athletics like dancing or gymnasts is an amazing tribute to the collaborative design of your body. Walking barefoot across the ground for example, uses 26 bones, 33 joints, and 100 muscles tendons and ligaments with each step. This does not include the incredible number of electrical messages continuously relayed amongst the brain, spinal cord, muscles and nerves needed to accomplish this seemingly simple action. A lot of information regarding mind and body can be gleaned about someone by watching them walk. Do they move with ease and fluidity or are they awkward or disjointed? Does their posture indicate an open heart? Do they walk with purpose or timidity?

Where does the heart fit into all of this? Research indicates your heart actually sends more messages to the brain than vice versa. Moreover, these messages are not just in the form of chemical messengers like peptides. The beating heart, for example, produces complex waves of energy, including sound and pressure, all of which influence the electrical activity of the brain. This creates a dynamic, synergistic relationship amongst your thoughts, emotions, physical body, subtle energy systems and the environment. This concept is generally ignored by most either because it does not seem important or does it fit with their ideas about how their bodyworks.

As mentioned in Part 1, humans have figured out how things work by the age of five. These ideas or naïve conceptions are highly resistant to change and persist throughout adulthood regardless of education, IQ and/or life-experience. Even more alarming, is that according to Mynatt et al (1979), these early perceptions of reality are so ingrained that even during a science experiment, students will change results to match their beliefs rather than re-evaluate their own. Students will commonly argue their experimental results were wrong because the class did not do the experiment correctly, or the teacher made a mistake and prepared the wrong chemicals.

For example, I often used a burning candle and a glass beaker to demonstrate the products of combustion. Heat and light energy are obvious products as is soot (carbon) because it leaves a black film on the bottom of the beaker. Capturing the smoke and bubbling it through limewater indicates production of carbon dioxide as well. So far so good, but the fine beads of moisture; which collect on the bottom of the glass frequently caused heated discussions! Water, according to a common naïve conception, cannot be formed by combustion because we use water to put out fire. Students have argued vehemently that if a burning candle produced water, then the flame would go out by itself therefore water cannot, be a product of combustion!

Apparently, even when you are engaged in an activity specifically designed to change a naïve conception it doesn't change without a struggle. This makes embracing a new perspective i.e. the ability of thoughts and intentions to alter your biochemistry all the more challenging. Another aspect of Pavlov's experiment, that is helpful, yet often unnoticed, is that the use of an external stimulus—in this case the ringing of the bell— causes an internal biochemical change i.e. the release of saliva in the conditioned dogs. Therefore, if the sound of a bell can trigger changes in physiology and behavior then it makes sense that thoughts and emotions impact your biochemistry as well. This parallels the cascade of biochemical changes sudden danger has on your autonomic nervous system.

In **7.1**, negative thoughts and emotions like frustration and anxiety were shown to produce incoherent heart rhythms while positive ones like gratitude and love, create smooth coherent ECGs (Fig. 21). According to James Oschmann, energetic pulses precede actions and provide a basis for thought. Consequently, thoughts or intentions should not be considered trivial because they give rise to specific patterns of electrical and magnetic activity in your heart and its ongoing dialogue with the nervous system.

In the early 1980's Louise Hay wrote *Heal your Body* as a guide for helping people use their thoughts and positive affirmations for re-patterning their mind. Significant evidence now supports her work and recent studies using MRI's of the brain for example, have shown repeated engagement in a specific behavior rewires the brain.

Donald Hebb, a neuropsychologist, believes *neurons that fire together wire together.* This begins when a particular thought or feeling triggers thousands of neurons; which form a neural network. As the repetitive thoughts, become ingrained, the brain learns to re-trigger these same patterns. If you keep complaining, criticizing, or worrying, the brain will revert to these neural networks more readily, even in a new situation or environment. In addition, the long-term consequences of such habits are strongly linked to numerous psychosomatic illnesses including cancer and heart disease. These same principles hold true for positive thoughts such as gratitude and compassion. Therefore, conscious focus upon positive, heart-centered thoughts and emotions shifts the following:

- your perspective of any event,
- your biochemistry,
- and helps re-pattern neural networks in the brain.

The overall result is a more vibrant sense of health and wellbeing.

This does not mean life challenges or difficult times disappear, but it does mean you will address them and cope from a more constructive perspective. Choosing heart-centered attitudes will help you *roll with the punches* and create greater resilience in all aspects of your being. Asking heart centered questions such as, "What can I learn from this situation?" or "How might I have done this in a more positive manner?" help steer you away from negative self-talk and destructive behaviors. Your past is not meant to define you and the practice of using heart-centered thoughts has many benefits. These benefits, and more, have been backed up by solid research some of it is based upon the electrical activity of your brain; which is the next topic.

8.2 Brainwaves and You

"Reality is built out of thought, and every
thought begins to create reality"
—Edgar Cayce

The brain is an astonishing organ. It collects and processes information, problem solves, creates order, provides coping skills, focuses attention, coordinates movement and so much more. The electrical activity of the brain creates energy fields similar to, albeit significantly smaller, than that of the heart as described in **5.6**. Just like your heart, the brain creates waves of electrical currents generated by the firing of thousands of neurons. These synchronized electrical signals can be detected outside the brain by placing electrodes on the scalp. Brainwaves are not the source or cause of brain states, they simply provide insights into what is being experienced at the time.

The first **electroencephalogram (EEG)**, designed by Hans Berger in 1929, was used to detect and measure these waves. Although it has become more sophisticated over the years the principles remain the same. **Fig.26** illustrates four of the five main phases of brainwaves. Based on their frequency, each phase represents different aspects of normal mental activity. They are described as follows:

1. **Delta:** the longest and slowest waves in the EEG, they range from 0.5 to 4 Hz in frequency. They are generated in dreamless sleep and the deepest meditation. Awareness of the outside world is suspended during this state whilst healing and rejuvenation are stimulated. These frequencies are associated with empathy and crucial to maintaining balanced mental, emotional and physical health.

2. **Theta:** these waves range from 4 to 8 Hz and are strongly detected when you are dreaming. They are also found during deep meditation and daydreaming. Theta is a twilight state, beyond normal conscious awareness, and associated with vivid imagery, intuition, and creativity. It can occur during an automatic task when the mind is disengaged e.g. washing dishes or brushing teeth.

3. **Alpha:** when you are physically and mentally relaxed, brainwaves between 8 and 13 Hz are detected. These frequencies are the

easiest to observe and the first to be discovered as they become evident when the eyes are closed and the mind is relaxed. They also occur just before falling asleep, when doing yoga or during artistic and creative activities. Alpha waves support overall mental coordination, calmness, alertness, mind/body integration and learning. They are associated with being present or in the moment.

4. **Beta:** these waves are associated with the *busy brain*. Ranging from 13 to 32 Hz they are generated when you are alert, conscious, and actively thinking. The lower end is associated with musing, the middle region with focusing on a task, while the high end is related to complex thought processes and excitement.

5. **Gamma:** the shortest, fastest, and most subtle brainwaves, they range from 32 to 100 Hz. Initially dismissed as *brain noise*, they are now associated with highly active states of altruism, universal love and heightened perception. They appear when peak processing from different brain areas occurs simultaneously, and is regularly observed in long time practitioners of meditation such as Buddhist Monks. Gamma frequencies are faster than the rate at which neurons can fire so how these waves are generated remains unknown. They appear to regulate perception and consciousness while individuals who show a greater presence of gamma brainwaves are more connected to states of expanded consciousness and spiritual experiences.

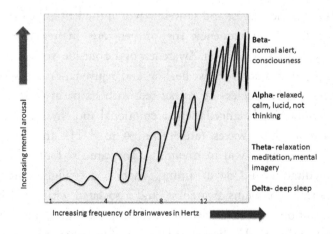

Diagram comparing the Frequency of Brainwaves as detected by an EEG to states of Mental Arousal

Brainwaves are actually more complex than described above. They can vary with how you are feeling and what you are doing. Slower waves reflect tired, slow dreamy states while higher frequencies occur when you are hyper-alert. Where the waves occur in the brain, what else is going on in the moment, and the current state of mental health all contribute to an EEG. Recently, another type of brainwave called **Infra-Low**, was discovered. Their slow nature makes them difficult to measure but they are believed to be a basic rhythm underlying higher brain functions and thought to play an important role in the ability of neurons to function as a network.

The extent and location of arousal in the brain has been linked to anxiety disorders, sleep issues, anger, and chronic pain while the lack of arousal in certain regions can lead to depression, attention deficit syndrome, and insomnia. Some issues may be a combination of these or other factors. Chemical interventions in the form of medications, and recreational drugs are more commonly used, although side effects are often an issue. Traditional eastern methods such as yoga and meditation were designed to train your brainwaves into balance and have become increasingly popular. Regardless, any process; which changes your perceptions, changes your brainwaves.

A newer method called **neurofeedback** has had considerable success at changing brainwaves as well. This technique is a type of biofeedback based on training your brain. Desireable brainwave frequencies are rewarded so, with practice, you can learn to regulate them. This training is so effective, NASA has used it as part of their astronaut-training program for over fifty years. In addition, athletes and businessmen use this type of training to facilitate peak performance and neurofeedback has been found useful in the treatment of ADHD, epilepsy and PTSD.

In a similar vein, certain healing traditions (e.g. Healing Touch) require the healer to prepare for their work using a heart-centered protocol that involves grounding and centering. Studies have shown that as the healer prepares to give a treatment, their brainwaves shift into an alpha and/ or an alpha-theta frequency of approximately 7 to 8 Hz. This is partially facilitated through training and practice of consciously connecting to the earth (grounding) and universe (centering). It is interesting to note that these frequencies are the same as those emanating from the earth. An exciting breakthrough which helped forge connections between science and energy medicine was the discovery, that at some point during a treatment, the client's brainwaves become entrained to those of the healer. It is not surprising that these frequencies--amongst others--are produced by some of the various electronic devices used in physical therapy settings.

The practice of **mindfulness** has gained considerable momentum in the scientific community as well. Multiple studies have confirmed it thickens the brain areas linked to the control of emotions and decision-making such as the **amygdala.** Mindfulness is associated with boosting the immune system too! David Cresswell from UCLA was the lead author on a study wherein subjects with HIV completed eight-weeks of mindfulness meditation training. At the end of the experiment, those who had completed the program had more CD-4T cells compared to those who did not take the training. The improved levels of these cells reflected greater immunity while the participants were able to slow the progression of the HIV virus.

Research, conducted by the Institute of HeartMath on **DHEA** (**dehydroepiandrosterone**) and cortisol showed parallel results to the HIV work. DHEA is a steroid hormone produced by the adrenal glands, gonads and the brain; which acts as an intermediate in the body's manufacture of steroids. DHEA is also involved with the growth and survival of both developing, and mature nerve cells. Experimental results showed that with as little as three minutes of meditation, DHEA levels increased by 100% while cortisol levels decreased by 23 %.

Earlier on, in Chapter 3, the effects of breathing upon your heart were discussed. According to current research, deep breathing can alter your brain activity. In one study, the breath work lasted from four to six minutes with the subjects breathing six breaths per minute. Each breath cycle began with a four second inhalation using the diaphragm, followed by two seconds of holding the breath and then four seconds of exhalation again using the diaphragm. This pattern increased the amount of alpha, theta and delta waves in the EEG of the participants. Normally when you are awake and thinking actively, you are in the beta frequencies. Having the ability to down shift to slower brain waves via breathing enables you to relax (and lower your stress responses) as well as, optimize learning and creativity. Who would have imagined the simple act of inhalation and exhalation could have such a powerful effect on your entire physiology, heart and mind!

Tuning into the origins of a message is an excellent tool for navigating your life. Generally, information originating in the brain is felt only in the head and is often associated with muscle tension and a sense or feeling being disconnected. Messages from the heart on the other hand are a full body experience. They may present as a jolt or goose bumps and all of your senses might feel more acutely aware. Sometimes you may hear, see, feel or know something without a rational explanation. Often these messages are subtle but with practice you can learn to distinguish between the two. One exercise that is helpful begins by paying attention to how you react to something you know is a lie. Then observe and compare what happens when you experience something you know was a good decision for you or another person at the time. Try being mindful or aware of your body's reaction to your answers as you complete Activity #9.

ACTIVITY #9

EXPLORING YOUR MINDFUL HEART

Objectives: This activity is intended to get you thinking about your personal attitudes regarding your thoughts and emotions. It will help you focus on those you want to work on with respect to re-patterning and/or shifting thoughts; which interfere with your ability to live fully and joyfully.

Begin by completing the following boxes in the chart shown for Fig. 23. Enter whatever issue(s) come to mind first. Try not to analyze it at first, but rather work from a heart-centered place within yourself. Take time to listen to how your body and mind react to the topics you choose to write down. Feel free to add other topics in the extra columns or make more charts if you have several topics you would like to explore now or at a later date. You do not have to fill in all the boxes now as you may find some don't fit for you or further inspiration may happen later on in the book or elsewhere. The phrase might shift as you move from one attitude to the next e.g. the first box might be answered based on the idea of "What makes me happy?" while under the next column Forgive, the question might be "What do I need to forgive?"

The final section is provided for you to write positive affirmations you can use to support the new positive patterns you are trying to establish in your life. You might for example, have written that looking at flowers make you happy and so your affirmation or action might be to look at a flower and smile for a few minutes every day.

Mindful Heart Record

	Happiness	Forgiveness	Gratitude	Compassion	Other
Positive Heart Thoughts:					
What					
When					
Where					
Why					
Who					
Affirmations/ Actions					

8.3 Happy Thoughts and You

"Happiness is not a destination to arrive at, but a way of travelling."
—Shakespeare.

When I was about 8 years old, I was given an autograph book and became enthused with collecting autographs from family and friends. One summer, at a family gathering, I got up the nerve to ask my cousins' grandmother for her autograph. She always appeared very stern and aloof so I was a little frightened of her although I attributed some of that to her battle with **Parkinson's**. She was sitting by herself under a beautiful shade tree as I walked over and asked her to sign my book. I was thrilled when she said yes and watched in anticipation as she painstakingly wrote the above quote from Shakespeare. When she finished I blushed as I thanked her and dashed off to read what she had written. At that time, I was somewhat confused by what I read. Most people wrote silly rhymes such as "Roses are red, violets are blue …" and I didn't quite understand what she had written meant. Later when I got up the courage to ask her she said that I would have to find that out for myself. Needless to say, it took a while for me to wrap my young mind around that concept but as the years passed and I experienced the roller coaster of my own life the truth of this simple phrase held more and more validity for me.

More often than not, most people believe they will be happy when they get *something* they want. This can range from very simple desires like ice cream for dessert or hugs from a loved one to more complicated goals such as landing the perfect job, finding their soul mate or winning the lottery. How often have you heard or used the phrase, "if only I had_____ I'd be happy". (What words would you use to fill in the blank?)

In his book *Happy City*, Charles Montgomery refers to **eudaimonia,** an ancient Greek ideology based on the belief that all humans can thrive by encouraging the infusion of good spirits. Good friends, health, fortune, power and material wealth were all significant aspects of eudaimonia and Greek cities were designed with the intention of fostering such assets. All citizens were considered a vital part of the city and contributed to common civic goals. Pure happiness, they believed, was only obtained by reaching the height of one's potential and that meant thinking and behaving in a virtuous manner.

Centuries later, as the Roman Empire expanded, and Greek culture faded, these inclusive ideals were marginalized. The grid design of the Roman city spanned three continents at its height and was welcomed for the security it provided. The Roman elite, however, focused on building monuments to celebrate their glory, while living conditions for the average Roman citizen deteriorated into intolerable slums. It is not a difficult leap of the imagination to understand how such actions sowed the seeds of discontent and unhappiness amongst the people.

Inevitably, as the Roman Empire declined and life became increasingly harsh greater numbers of people began to look elsewhere for happiness. Magnificent places of worship were frequently built to provide communities with the solace and empathy people needed. These edifices were designed to guide one's gaze toward heaven and the promise of happiness in the afterlife. Hence, they became the new "heart of the city".

For the last two hundred years or so, western economists have chosen to use the purchase of goods and services as the primary indicator of a population's happiness. This index is based on the misleading assumption that the more money people spend on things the happier they are. Somehow, material wealth became a barometer of happiness in today's society. So much so that many people postpone happiness until they have their dream home, pay off their mortgage or have a certain amount of money in the bank.

Financial wealth is often pursued, as a means to happiness even though research has shown wealthy people are no happier than the rest of the population. According to the August 2015 issue of *Scientific Mind*, how you spend your money influences your happiness. For example, people are happier when they spend their money on experiences such as travel or concerts rather than merchandise. Anticipation of an event, plus the enjoyment of the experience, keeps your levels of **dopamine** elevated for a much longer period of time than the instant gratification obtained when you buy something such as a burger or a new item of clothing. Associated with our moods, motivation and reward systems, dopamine is structurally related to epinephrine and norepinephrine. Secreted mostly by the brain and the gut, low levels of this vital neurotransmitter have been related to depression and neurological conditions such as Parkinson's and Multiple Sclerosis.

How do you really know when you are happy? Specific **biomarkers** for the measurement of happiness are still elusive and, although people are not always certain if they are happy or not, scientists do know that you have a cascade of messengers including serotonin, oxytocin, dopamine, endorphins, and other peptides which are involved in our ability to *feel* good. More importantly, there is significant evidence linking these chemicals to your heart and overall health.

Despite a lack of definitive biomarkers for happiness, people definitely know when or if they are unhappy. Many studies have shown a significant correlation between elevated levels of cortisol in the saliva and depression (perceived unhappiness). **Cortisol**, a hormone released by the adrenal gland when you are under stress and directly stimulates your SNS. Cortisol causes significant strains on the physical body and has been shown to lead to: weight gain, hypertension, sleep issues, musculoskeletal pain, increased health risk behavior (e.g. alcohol and tobacco abuse) and mental health issues such as anxiety and depression. Thus it follows that the greater your resilience and ability to deal with stress, the lower your cortisol levels and the happier you are. The question then becomes how do you nurture resilience and elevate happiness?

Trying to be happier seems to backfire as happiness can't be forced and worrying about your happiness can cause even more unhappiness. Planning to spend some of your time doing things you enjoy on a regular basis such as gardening, socializing, sports etc., can help you become more satisfied with your life in general and increase resilience. Studies have shown the simple act of remembering a time when you were happy changes your heart rate, respiration, and blood pressure. Happy thoughts also stimulate your PNS and lower cortisol levels. Of equal significance is the study done by Jain et al (2011) that demonstrated gentle energy treatments such as Reiki or Healing Touch reduced salivary cortisol levels. Indicating that relaxation or stimulation of the PNS was taking place.

Many look to love and marriage as a solution to happiness. According to Robert Holden, author of *Be Happy*, a study, of 24,000 couples observed over fifteen years revealed that couples in long-term relationships had higher happiness scores. No surprise there, but it was surprising that those with the highest happiness scores were already happy before they entered their relationship. Evidently, if you are not already happy, finding your *true love* is not going to make you any happier in the long run. In fact, cancel any and all expectations of someone else making you happy, as it will invariably set you up for disappointment. Moreover as Holden states, "to be happy you have to give up all hope of having a better past!"

When I was growing up our family subscribed to the *Reader's Digest*. My favorite section was called "Laughter the Best Medicine" which contained many humorous jokes and stories. Not only did they make me laugh, they provided jokes etc., to share at family gatherings. Most everyone excelled at telling jokes or funny stories; which kept everyone laughing. When someone was feeling blue, our mother frequently said "Laugh and the world laughs with you. Cry and you cry alone." Then she would share a funny story or a joke.

For the most part, humor was simply part of our family dynamics and I didn't really think much about it in a formal sense. Nonetheless, I have always sensed that keeping my sense of humor was an important tool as a teacher and often added a joke or cartoon to my lessons to brighten everyone's mood. Now there is considerable evidence; which supports the importance of laughter and its ability to help you relax. Laughter also improves your ability to learn and remember--and should be part of every teacher's tool kit. If you appreciate how difficult it is to furrow your brow or turn down your mouth when you are laughing, it is not so farfetched to embrace humor as an opportunity to turn on those positive chemicals; which make you happy.

The popularity of laughter never wanes either and many old films are a true gift from many great comedians such as Bob Hope, Robin Williams, and Jim Carrey. Not only is laughter contagious, forcing yourself to laugh even when you don't feel like it will trigger real laughter. Laughter is also healing. Hob Osterlund a pain and palliative care specialist researched the impact of comedy on the symptoms of cancer and chemotherapy. The results not only demonstrated humor had a positive effect, she went on to create comedy programming for hospital closed-circuit televisions called the *Chuckle Channel* which has helped speed the recovery of many. Additionally, an organization called Laughter Yoga has become very popular, and its classes have made a difference in helping people to feel happier

Oh yes, and let's not forget music! According to a recent article in the science and technology section of Mail Online, a group of neuroscientists, analyzed music from the last 50 years in search of the components that made people feel good. They discovered that using a high tempo (150 beats per minute), a third major key and holiday type lyrics were integral to music that elevated the listener's mood. They listed the top ten songs of all time and the number one spot goes to, "Don't Stop Me Now" by Queen followed by Abba's "Dancing Queen." So if you don't feel like watching a comedy, reading a joke book or practicing laughter yoga then go to the link below, crank up the tunes and let the good times roll!

http://www.dailymail.co.uk/sciencetech/article-3238679/Queen-s-Don-t-Stop-feel-good-song-past-50-years-scientific-formula-proved-it.html

8.4 Forgiveness and You

"The truth is unless you let go, unless you forgive yourself, unless you forgive the situation, unless you realize that the situation is over, you cannot move forward."
—Steve Maraboli

Extracting DNA was a popular lab with students. Basically it involves mashing up some living material in a salty soap solution. Strawberries, broccoli, spinach or peas work quite well. After filtering out the solid particles alcohol is slowly added to the filtered solution. A fine white stringy material collects in a layer where the two solutions meet which can be wound out on a stick. This is DNA—the blueprint of life!

In 1865, Gregor Mendel proposed the basic principles of inheritance. For example, every person inherits two sets of DNA, one from each parent. The expression of genetic traits such as eye color or blood type was initially thought to be determined through the principles of dominance and recession between the two sets of DNA. Sometimes parts of the DNA are defective and genetic testing can be used to locate those sections of DNA responsible for the problems. In some cases, the DNA can be repaired and this is happening in more and more situations. Such work is incredible and has helped many people. Amazing as it is, scientists have found that genetics does not ha ve exclusive rights to health and healing. DNA is not destiny.

Studies of identical twins, have demonstrated the profound influence other factors have on the expression of identical DNA. For example, one twin who works out regularly will have a completely different physique that the other twin who does not. Diet, employment, relationships etc., all impact the expression DNA. Many traits are expressed via a collaborative effort amongst DNA, the environment, and choices. Additionally, there is a myriad of molecules associated with DNA that participate in the process of which genes are turned on or off. The study of this process is called **epigenetics** and has revolutionized the understanding of inheritance. Emotions, and thoughts have been found to play crucial roles in the epigenetics of wellness especially those of forgiveness and gratitude.

Marianne Williamson describes forgiveness as the greatest healer and the ultimate in preventative medicine. Medical doctors are beginning to acknowledge that patients who refuse to forgive often stay sick. Holding on to negative emotions, thoughts and memories such as anger, resentment and hatred create a state of chronic anxiety that ripple throughout your personal ecosystem. Forgiving someone, or a group of people that have hurt you badly is certainly one of life's most challenging tasks. Yet, unless you choose to forgive you will carry this bitterness to your grave.

Unfortunately, forgiveness does not happen with mere lip service or blithely telling yourself or another person you forgive them. Nor does it mean you condone the hurtful or violent actions of others. Forgiveness does not mean the perpetrator of your hurt will ever apologize or repent especially if they are narcissistic or deceased. In order to forgive however, you must make a choice to dig beneath your pain, ego or pride and connect with the core of your psyche. Nurture this core with unconditional love for yourself every day!

You may want to journal who and what you want to forgive--beginning with yourself. Mistakes, judgments, harsh deeds and so on; whatever keeps you from being kinder to yourself. As you evolve in your ability to love and forgive yourself, you can begin your work on forgiving others including those who are deceased. This too may be done via journaling, meditation, drawing etc. Try positive affirmation while standing in front of a mirror, look yourself in the eye and state out loud "I am loved, I am worthy, I am beautiful, I am competent etc.

True forgiveness is liberating and brings a sense of empowerment. But, remember that until time machines are perfected, you cannot change the past no matter how hard you try! Forgiving others releases the burdens of pain, anger and other negative emotions; which can literally make you sick. According to C.S Lewis,

> *"Getting over a painful experience is much like crossing the monkey bars, you have to let go at some point in order to move forward"*

A few years ago, Justin St.Vincent compiled an inspiring book called *Love, Live, Forgive*. Published in New Zealand, it is a collection of the thoughts and experiences of many famous recording artists on this topic and how it is reflected in their work. Here is the link:

http://www.loveliveforgive.org

Furthermore, you may find the following guided meditations on this topic helpful:

https://jeannettenienaber.bandcamp.com/album/love-forgiveness-joy

8.5 Gratitude and You

"Be content with what you have; rejoice in the way things are. When you realize there is nothing lacking, the whole world belongs to you."
—Lao Tzu

Everyone, from toddlers to seniors, likes to be thanked for what they do. Receiving an expression of gratitude always makes you feel better. Thanking someone or being thanked goes way beyond the idea of a polite social nicety, in fact, it has profound effects on everyone's overall quality of life. It somehow brings into balance the energies of heart and mind. Moreover, there is evidence to back this up! Several studies have demonstrated that those who practice gratitude have more peaceful and fulfilling lives than those who are ungrateful, jealous, resentful etc.

What most do not realize is that gratitude is attitude with chemistry! Each time you consciously choose to be grateful, your body activates the reward system in your brain to release dopamine. As mentioned in **8.3**, dopamine is a key player in your body's reward system. It not only lets you know when you have done something good, it helps you remember so you can get rewarded again! Low levels of dopamine, in contrast, are associated with memory loss, dullness, depression, and loss of coordination in certain muscle groups. The antidepressant Wellbutrin for example, is designed to boost your levels of dopamine but it is not a cure for depression.

Neurons containing tiny black dots can be found in an area of your midbrain called the **substantia nigra** (Fig. 24). These neurons are your body's main source of dopamine; which is synthesized from the amino acid tyrosine (Fig. 2). Their dark color is due to a pigment called **neuromelanin** whose function is not well understood at this time. Recent studies however, have shown that when dopamine receptors are blocked, the functions of the heart peptide ANP (**6.6**) is impaired. Considering gratitude is also a choice that alters brain waves and improves heart coherence, adding dopamine to the equation provides another example of the incredible web of subtle interconnections amongst the heart and brain. So when you think you have nothing to be grateful for you can always check your pulse!

After a particularly busy time, it's important to slow down the firing of those neurons in your mind so you can experience some calmness and peace. This is the role of two important neurotransmitters **GABA (gamma amino butyric acid)** and **serotonin.** GABA helps neurons recover after firing hence it acts to *cool down* the engines of your mind. It regulates norepinephrine, epinephrine, dopamine and serotonin; thus it is intimately involved with mood regulation and has been referred to as mother nature's sedative. Most prescription sleep aids, sedatives and tranquilizers work via the GABA system as it reduces anxiety and worry.

Often deemed the master neurotransmitter, serotonin contributes to your feelings of self-worth, happiness, and general wellbeing in addition to being closely linked to the physiology of sleep, appetite, pain management, and digestion. Erosion of healthy serotonin levels can be caused by high stress, sleep deprivation, poor nutrition, and inflammation often resulting in depression, anxiety and other mood disorders. Oh but wait there is more! Practicing gratitude boosts serotonin levels. Gratitude opens your heart to giving and receiving love and helps you transcend suffering by bringing you peace; which is facilitated by dopamine, GABA and serotonin.

Your heart's production of endorphins and peptides such as oxytocin were topics of Chapters 6 & 7; which laid the groundwork for how your heart influences your mind and emotions. This chapter has looked at the interactions between the mind and heart in more depth and has demonstrated the value of exercise, mindfulness, meditation, and positive choices for enhanced living. Humans need to practice self-love, compassion, forgiveness and gratitude to optimize their built in reward systems. The final section of this chapter takes a closer look at how your choices influence your ability to thrive.

8.6 Choices and You

"The one power that can literally change the future: your power of choice...each choice you make can bring you into partnership with the divine in the sacred process of co-creation."
—Caroline Myss

According to many therapists such as Georgina Cannon, how you interact with others in relationships is reflected on how you interact with yourself. All aspects and all walks of life dish out many different interactions. Some are messy and dysfunctional—often in families—and others are connected and joyful. The good news you get to choose!

Sometimes it seems as if you are locked into a position or situation that is miserable with no way out. At this point it becomes imperative to remember there is always a way out it's just that sometimes, deep down inside, you don't want to or think you can't make that choice for whatever reason. You may think you don't deserve a better boss or that you are not smart enough to achieve your dreams. Such thoughts are self-limiting and many are passed on from parents to children for generations. As previously discussed, such thoughts can be rewired by learning to become aware of and choosing strategies that help you counteract these self-sabotaging patterns. However, it is important to remember that not deciding still means you have made a choice.

People feel empowered and have a greater sense of freedom when they are allowed to choose. This translates to children as well. When they are told what to do or not to do, they become contrary at any age but especially so as teenagers. If they are given a choice, both of which you can live with, then it is a win/win scenario. For example asking them if they would rather clean up the dishes from dinner or put away their laundry is usually more constructive than telling them to do one or the other. The same can work with a friend or partner e.g. would you like to go for a walk or out to lunch? There are always more difficult situations than described but developing creative choice strategies can be an effective way to engage others in a mutually beneficial relationship.

Nevertheless, some people, no matter how hard you try may not be ready for your energy. When this happens, you must set priorities and boundaries about what you will and will not permit others to do or say to you. You can choose whether or not this relationship is valuable to you. Moreover, this can be done in a positive way by choosing to take the high road. Refuse to let them engage you in negative thoughts and emotions that are based in anger, hatred, fear or frustration. They only serve to rewire your brain and heart into self-destructive patterns. Send them your best wishes either in person or mentally as much and as often as you need to and move on!

The well-known Cherokee legend called *Two Wolves* may be familiar to you and is a good reminder of the internal battles and choices faced by everyone.

> *"An old Cherokee is teaching his grandson about life. "A fight is going on inside me," he said to the boy. "It is a terrible fight and it is between two wolves. One is evil—he is anger, envy, sorrow, regret, greed, arrogance, self-pity, guilt, resentment, inferiority, lies, false pride, superiority, and ego." He continued, "the other is good—he is joy, peace, love, hope, serenity, humility, kindness, benev9lence, empathy, generosity, truth, compassion and faith. The same fight is going on inside you—and inside every other person, too."*
>
> *The grandson thought about it for a minute and then asked his grandfather, "Which wolf will win?"*
>
> *The old Cherokee simply replied, "The one you feed."*

Believe it or not, stress too can be a choice. When confronted with a potentially stressful situation, such as moving, a new job, divorce, etc., it is particularly important to find effective strategies. Go back through your answers and thoughts to some of the activities you have done throughout this book. Find ways to practice forgiveness and gratitude; exercise or meditate--anything to help your ANS move into its calmer vegetative modes. Practice, practice, practice so that you can be present and in the moment with grace and ease. Confiding in others and seeking support from both friends and professionals is also important during challenging times. Remember your past mistakes are meant to guide you not define you.

One more thing--research in the areas of biofeedback and brain state training demonstrate that the more you are self-aware, the more they can interact with yourself in a positive manner. The rule of thumb for making any personal change is to stay on track for 90 days. After 90 days, it becomes a habit. Consider what your action plans for change embody! The following list summarizes constructive strategies discussed in Your Mindful Heart. You may like to add some of your own and post a copy on your fridge or desktop as a reminder!

1. Choose to love yourself as much as you want to be loved
2. Plan short term pleasures and long-term goals
3. Find time to be with positive friends on a regular basis
4. Limit stressful events, social media, and smartphone access
5. Choose positive thoughts and happiness over negative ones and anxiety
6. Remind yourself to be grateful even for small things
7. Take long slow deep breaths several times a day
8. Remember to exercise, meditate, sleep, play and laugh
9. Forgive yourself and others
10. Practice letting go of all that does not serve you
11. Choose to remember the good times rather than the bad
12. Listen to the wisdom of your heart
13. Strive to find a sense of meaning and purpose in your life
14. Seek continued personal growth and a sense of independence
15. Find and learn from great teachers

In summary, Part 4 has brought forward concepts and evidence regarding the dynamics amongst your heart and mind. Much of the current research indicates the crucial importance of doing your own work. This includes developing self-awareness of emotions, thoughts and choices as a means of personal empowerment. Knowledge is considered the process of gathering information, while the perception of knowledge is wisdom. Engaging the heart balances IQ (intelligence quotient) with EQ (emotional intelligence quotient). Therefore, the more you trust your heart's intuitive ability, the greater your connection with its innate wisdom.

The segue to this work begins with connecting to something more, something beyond the *normal* range of information relayed to the brain by eyes, ears, nose, mouth and skin. Something that has been described for eons in many different ways yet continues to elude description. That *something* will be explored in Part 5 and is eloquently expressed by Van Morrison,

> *"If my heart could do my thinking*
> *And my head begin to feel*
> *I would look upon the world anew*
> *And know what's truly real".*

PART 5

YOUR SPIRITUAL HEART

"Because Divine energy is inherent in our biological system, every thought that crosses our minds, every belief we nurture ...translates into a positive or negative command to our bodies and spirits."
—Caroline Myss

Overview

Buoyancy of spirit, the ability to persevere despite hardship, and a strong belief in *something more* is the stuff of heroes and saviors. Thousands of stories about such archetypes, spanning eons of human existence, can be found throughout all cultures. Incredible monuments, statues, and buildings have been built around the globe to honor these people. Where might the source of such inner strength reside? What are the personal tools needed to create your own foundation?

Part 5 braids the previous themes of this book into contemplation of your spiritual heart. Discussion begins with the fundamental roles of hope, awe and compassion towards the construction of a robust spiritual heart. This leads to a deeper look at the ecology of your heart thru the lens of an ancient Buddhist principle called The Empty Circle or **Pratîtya-Samutpâda-âdi**. Consideration of this principle, and the insights it reveals, amongst science, you and your heart are pursued as your spiritual heart is illuminated in the final chapter.

CHAPTER 9

METAMORPHOSIS

9.1 Hope and You

> *"Hope springs eternal in the human breast;*
> *Man never is, but always To be blest.*
> *The soul, uneasy, and confin'd from home,*
> *Rests and expatiates in a life to come."*
> **—Alexander Pope**

I recall my father telling me one of things he loved about our mother was her optimistic spirit. After growing up during The Great Depression (1929-1939) and then living through WW II (1939 to 1945), he said it was hard to find people who tried to look on the brighter side of life. Their entire generation was scarred by personal tragedy in one way or another and many suffered from undiagnosed anxiety, depression, and other symptoms of PTSD; which was barely known in those days.

In his later years, my father had always wanted to die on the golf course from a fatal heart attack. In fact, that's actually what happened. However, he was revived and sent to hospital. After several weeks, an anti-arrhythmic heart drug was found to regulate his heartbeat. Soon he was back on the golf course but a few months later, on a hot August day, he was struggling for his breath. Initially diagnosed with pneumonia (in August?) it was eventually discovered he was allergic to his anti-arrhythmic drug. By that time, 95% of his lung function was lost due to fibrosis. He survived another five harsh years through the love and hope showered upon by him by devoted family and friends. Then one day his optimism disappeared. The doctor had told him there was *no hope left* and abruptly, his transition towards death began.

Thousands of stories regarding the impact of hope upon the human spirit have been told. For eons, humans have overcome horrendous, unimaginable odds through the tenacity of their courage and hope. Thus the value of hope can never be underestimated. More importantly, it allows us to thrive, dream and strive for a better life. Lack of hope, on the other hand, sends people downward into despair, fear, and pessimism. It makes humans bitter and judgmental and often drives them to commit hateful acts. I have yet to see *hope* packaged in shrink-wrap in the grocery store--so where does it come from?

Viktor Frankl was a Jewish psychiatrist, imprisoned in concentration camps during the Nazi regime. Despite horrific conditions he strove to observe and record his thoughts and experiences; which appear in his book *Man's Search for Meaning*. His description of how he encouraged others to hope has carried me through difficult times and I have included it here with the hope that it may inspire you as well:

"On the evening of this day of fasting we lay in our earthen huts—in a very low mood. Very little was said and every word sounded irritable. Then, to make matters even worse the light went out. Tempers reached their lowest ebb. But our senior block warden was a wise man. He improvised a little talk about the many comrades who had died in the last few days, either of sickness or of suicide. But he also mentioned what may have been the real reason for their deaths: giving up hope. He maintained that there should be some way of preventing possible future victims from reaching this extreme And it was to me that the warden pointed to give this advice.

God knows, I was not in the mood to give psychological explanations or to preach any sermons—to offer my comrades a kind of medical care of their souls.

I was cold and hungry, irritable and tired, but I had to make the effort and use this unique opportunity. Encouragement was now more necessary than ever.

So I began by mentioning the most trivial of comforts first. I said that even in the Europe in the sixth winter of the Second World War, our situation was not the most terrible we could think of. I said that each of us had to ask himself what irreplaceable losses he had suffered up to then. I speculated that for most of them these losses had really been few. Whoever was still alive had reason for hope. Health, family, happiness, professional abilities, fortune, position in society—all these were things that could be achieved again or restored. After all, we still had all our bones intact. Whatever we had gone through could still be an asset to us in the future. And I quoted from Nietzsche: 'wasmmich nicht umbrinft, macht mich starker.' (That which does not kill me, makes me stronger.)...

Then I spoke of the many opportunities of giving life a meaning. I told my comrades (who lay motionless although occasionally a sigh could be heard) that human life, under any circumstances, never ceases to have a meaning, and that this infinite meaning of life includes suffering and dying, privation and death. I asked the poor creatures who listened to me attentively in the darkness of the hut to face up to the seriousness of our position. They must not lose hope but should keep their courage in the certainty that the hopelessness of our struggle did not detract from its dignity and its meaning. I said that someone looks down on each of us in difficult hours—a friend, a wife, somebody alive or dead, or a God—and he would not expect us to disappoint him. He would hope to find us suffering proudly—not miserably—knowing how to die."

At the onset of the 21st Century, my parents were in their eighties and for the last ten years both had endured a litany of serious health issues--even dodged death on several occasions. As the New Year approached they choose to attend a huge celebration with their friends despite dire predictions about the end of the world. They had lived and loved through several Armageddon's both real and imagined yet still chose optimism and hope. Their courage and belief in *something more* will always be an inspiration to me. Activity #10, which follows, is designed to help you reflect upon various facets of your spiritual heart.

ACTIVITY #10

EXPLORING YOUR SPIRITUAL HEART

Objectives: Think of this exercise as a guided tour to help you consolidate who you are and what you believe in. Such reflections are pivotal to establishing the personal clarity and awareness that are foundational to building inner spiritual strength and integrity.

Part A: Begin by answering each of the following questions as honestly as you can. The first thoughts that come to mind are usually the best ones to choose rather than over thinking the questions. You may choose to do this work in whatever manner appeals to you the most e.g. record you answers in this book, write/draw in your journal or voice record etc.

1. What, or who, brings you hope and how does that feel?

2. When (if ever) have you felt things or life were hopeless? What else was going on in your life at this time?

3. What or who brings awe and magic to your life? How does experiencing awe affect you?

4. What does compassion mean to you? How does the experience of compassion feel for you?

5. In what ways do you practice self-compassion? In what ways do you practice compassion for others?

6. What does your spiritual heart want you to know at this time?

Part B: When you feel your answers to Part A are complete, contemplate 1 or 2 action plans that you would like to set in place with respect to nurturing your spiritual heart with the gifts of hope, awe and compassion.

Plan 1:

Plan 2:

You may wish to revisit these thoughts and plans in the days and months after you have finished reading this book as you engage in the synergy of your own personal evolution--physically, emotionally, mentally and spiritually.

9.2 Awe and You

> *"To see the World in a Grain of Sand*
> *And a Heaven in a Wild Flower*
> *Hold Infinity in the palm of your hand*
> *And Eternity in an hour..."*
> **—William Blake**

One of the reasons children are so delightful is their sense of wonder. It is easy to amaze and surprise them with seemingly everyday things like a spoon or a drop of water. As true beginners, they explore the world thru fresh senses--captivated by the mystery of creation. They are powerful reminders of the eloquent beauty in the cycle of life. Finding the gift, or the lesson for each experience--both positive and negative--elevates the spirit and galvanizes a sense of awe for all that is.

Along a similar line, Stellar (2015) measured the frequency with which people agreed or disagreed with statements regarding their experiences of awe, joy, wonder, contentment, and pride. Using statements such as "I feel wonder almost every day", or I am an intensely cheerful person" she found that those who regularly experienced high levels of these positive emotions had significantly lower levels of a molecule responsible for signaling inflammation (**interleukin-6**). Moreover, group analysis revealed that experiences of awe produced the lowest levels of interleukin-6--lending even more credibility to the importance savoring the enchantment and magic of the universe.

Some 30 years ago or so if you had told me that I would choose to leave a successful teaching career to work as an energy healer, I would probably have scoffed and thought you were quite absurd. At that time, although curious about the unexplained, I still believed science held the all answers. Then, in my early forties, I had a Near Death Experience and everything changed.

I remember lying in the corridor of the emergency room so exhausted and in such pain that I didn't want to try anymore. A lingering abscess—a legacy from childbirth—had burst for the fourth time. I was in horrible pain, septic and began to pray for death. As I craved release from my earthly existence, the chaos of the ER, and the horrid sensations in my body began to fade from my awareness. I felt myself lifting upwards, floating on beautiful clouds. I started to feel liberated and joyful--my prayers were being answered!

As I floated upwards, I was filled with peace and love. I could see my body below me and did not long for it as I drifted towards a tunnel filled with the most incredible light, loving spirits and music. A rapid panorama of my life's journey began to flow through my consciousness--like a movie. When the screen came to the birth of each of my sons I suddenly realized how much they still needed me. I panicked and began to beg and pray to go back. Saying over and over again that I had to stay to and raise my children.

I have no idea of how much time passed then abruptly I heard a powerful voice say, "You will live! They will operate in four days." Instantly, I was back in my body, and saw my neighbor Dr. Grady McNeilly tapping me to wake me up. As I became conscious, he began to place orders to the nurses etc., to take care of me. He told me my eldest son, Ryan, had called and asked if he could bring his little brothers, Darren and Sean, to their house because I had gone to emergency. Grady immediately dashed to the hospital as his wife Glenda, scooped up my boys who were 9, 7 and 5 at the time.

Some twenty-five years later, I am still in awe of, and extremely grateful, for the amazing support we received from neighbors, friends and colleagues as they stepped in to care for my sons until my sister and mother could arrive. Things were complicated, as my father had just undergone heart surgery. Obviously, this experience changed much of my attitude to life forever. Most notably, was the utter conviction that we are all souls—divine beings--having a human experience. This belief constantly reminds me to be grateful for everyday miracles. It fuels hope, compassion and love for the mystery of life. It really doesn't get any more awesome than that!

9.3 Compassion and You

"If I told patients to raise their blood levels of immune globulins or T-cells no one would know how. But if I told them to love themselves and others fully the same change happens automatically."
—Bernie Siegel

People express love in many different ways to friends, family, colleagues and others. Words such as warmhearted, kind-hearted, merciful and compassionate are often used to describe those who can put their ego aside and truly open their heart towards others. The word compassion actually means to *suffer together*. When you are confronted with another's suffering, and feel motivated to relieve that suffering you are experiencing compassion. The practice of unconditional love and attainment of inner peace for self are essential pre-requisites for cultivating a compassionate heart. According to Anne Frank,

> *"When you find peace within yourself, you become the kind of person who can live at peace with others."*

To attain inner peace and work from a compassionate heart, you must first be fine-tuned with unconditional love for yourself. This is an ongoing, often difficult process for most; especially those who have never received or experienced unconditional love. (Many of the activities in this book were designed to support such personal evolution). The second phase of developing the compassionate heart involves the practice of unconditional love for others. This means to love another person without judgment, control or a personal agenda. It also demands full acceptance of a person or situation; regardless of the outcome. This too is an arduous task partly because it is human nature to hang out with others who have similar interests and who think and believe along the same lines. Such associations often bring external confirmation and comfort about your way of life and the feelings of belonging; which is akin to finding your tribe.

Tribal difficulties arise when individuals do not fit the perceived status quo of a tribe. Different perceptions and disagreements regarding faith, how the world works, or what and how things should be done often lead to racism, hatred and war. After the assassination of Martin Luther King Jr. in April 1948, Jane Elliot strove to find a meaningful lesson for her elementary students centered on tribalism. Her famous *Brown Eyes and Blue Eyes Racism Experiment* was the result. It continues to serve as an excellent example of how clustering beliefs in a tribal like setting overrides the human expressions of empathy and compassion. Fear in its many forms prevails against and further justifies discrimination for those that are different.

A link to Jane Elliot's, *Brown Eyes and Blue Eyes Racism Experiment* can be found here:

https://www.youtube.com/watch?v=KHxFuO2Nk-0

Although the concepts of empathy and altruism are related to compassion, they are not the same. Empathy refers to your ability to take the perspective of and/or feel the emotions of another person—try walking in their shoes! Compassion occurs when those feelings and thoughts include the desire to help. While altruism, on the other hand, is kind, selfless behavior but it isn't always motivated by compassion. Additionally, you can feel compassion for others without acting on it.

Recent studies regarding the biological basis of compassion show it is deeply rooted in our evolution and ability to survive as a species. Feelings of compassion slow your heart rate, and increase the secretion of oxytocin; which simultaneously enhances bonding and attachment as previously described in **6.1.** As well as this, areas of the brain linked to pleasure, empathy and nurturing light up when you are experiencing compassion. Together, these subtle, yet significant biochemical shifts, stimulate a deep desire to support and care for others—characteristics of a heart centered person.

Your heart chakra--an energy vortex found in the center of the chest--is considered a unique part of the human energy system because it acts as a link between the lower and upper chakras. When you can freely express the frequencies of unconditional love and compassion, the heart chakra acts like a transformer. It enables you to link the lower chakras of the physical world with the upper chakras of the subtle mysteries. In a sense, heaven and earth interface through your heart in an ongoing dialogue. Part of this dialogue includes the information exchange between your heart and brain. Buried deep within the brain, just above the brainstem and underneath the cerebral cortex (Fig. 4) is the **limbic** system. This group coordinates behavioral and emotional responses on numerous levels and includes the following structures: thalamus, hypothalamus, basal ganglia, hippocampus and amygdala.

Wallentin et al (2011) observed the emotional responses in the brain of subjects listening to a story. Areas of the brain; which lit up when the subjects experienced strong emotions, were detected using **functional magnetic resonance imaging (fMRI)**. This data was dovetailed with measurements of heart rate variability (HRV). A strong, positive, correlation was found between emotional changes and activation of the amygdala (and other areas of the limbic system). Moreover, these changes were directly parallel to changes in the HRV. In other words, your emotional experiences are directly associated with changes in your heart rate and brain activity. No wonder it is so hard to think clearly or make good decisions when you are angry or sad etc.!

Such research indicates the communication between your heart and mind is of a much more complex nature. The limbic system is anatomically located in the region of the brow chakra--commonly referred to the as the third eye—which is associated with the pituitary gland. This region is connected with intuition especially that of clairvoyance. Further research along these lines may lead to additional insights regarding the development of intuition and spiritual experiences.

Throughout history, many traditions have developed paths for achieving heightened states of awareness. All of the great religions of the world promote the practice of meditation or prayer along with the cultivation of unconditional love and compassion as a means of attaining enlightenment. All spiritual experiences are associated with a perceived sense of connection; which transcends the ordinary sense of self.

Obviously, these experiences impact the brain and were recently studied by a team from Columbia and Yale universities. According to Miller et al (2018) subjects experiencing personally meaningful spiritual experiences showed reduced activity in a part of their brain called the **left inferior parietal lobe (IPL)**. This area influences attention and is believed responsible for spatial orientation, sensations, and language. Researchers also found the spiritual experience itself; was more important than what actually triggers the event. Therefore, regardless of whether the subjects were communing with nature, their church, or a stadium full of sports fans the effect on the brain appears to be the same. Furthermore, this effect is distinctly different from the brain's relaxation response--even though relaxation may be an important preliminary step towards transcendence.

Other studies have shown that the neural pathways and regions of the brain associated with analytical and rational thought, are separate and distinct from those linked to spiritual and empathic processes. Tony Jack, director of the Brain, Mind, and Consciousness lab, suggests that because spiritual and analytical thinking do not occur simultaneously in the brain, both modes need to be cultivated for optimal health and wellness. Such thoughts give even more credibility when considered in the light of ancient traditions such as yoga.

The word yoga means, "bliss" and its practice, facilitates the fusion of mind and body to form a unity. This unity lays the foundation for processes; which heighten intuition and lead to transcendent states. In Section III of the *Yoga Sutras* miraculous yogic powers called vibhutis and siddhis are mentioned. However, in *Autobiography of a Yogi,* the author P. Yogananda, cautions that although true knowledge or analytical thinking is always power, the sole pursuit of vibhutis and siddhis should not be your Infinite Goal. Instead you must strive towards unity with spirit. When you have mastered this transcendent state, you can choose to use your powers or not, from a place of infinite wisdom and compassion.

Achievement of such a level of awareness is not attained with ease. It is the essence of all great spiritual leaders and according to Annette Duveroth it is,

> *"In total surrender of the ego, the transformation of our vibration unfolds by itself, to levels far beyond our imagination."*

Yogananda elaborates this further when he implies that when you have attained such a level of egoless awareness, all actions, miraculous or otherwise, are then performed without karmic involvement. He goes on to state, … "the iron filings of karma are attracted only where a magnet of the personal ego still exists." In other words, it's not all about you. You need to cultivate all of your heart's physical, emotional, mental and spiritual gifts. Nurture the gifts of unconditional love, happiness, forgiveness, gratitude, hope, awe, and compassion and finally, surrender to *something more.*

9.4 The Empty Circle and You: Pratîtya-Samutpâda-âdi.

> *"My soul counseled me and instructed me so that*
> *the light which I carry is not my light,*
> *That the song was not created within me.*
> *For though I travel with the light, I am not the light.*
> *And though I am a lute fastened with*
> *strings, I am not the lute player."*
> **—Kabril Gibran**

The word *Namaste* encapsulates the beauty of the spiritual heart. It means my soul recognizes your soul. That I honor the light, love, breath, truth, and kindness within you because it is also within me, in sharing these things there is no distance and no difference. We are one.

In the Tibetan Buddhist tradition there is a doctrine known as the Empty Circle or **Pratîtya-Samutpáda-ádi.** Anchored by the concepts of wholeness, its ideas were brought forward by Vasubandu circa 400 AD. The image of an empty circle; symbolizes the dualistic viewpoint of *everything and nothing* and is often used as a mandala for meditation.

Fig. 27 The Empty Circle--a metaphor for Dependent Co-origination

In the ecology of existence, everything is related, to everything else and all things are believed to co-create the universe. The belief that *when this exists, that exists*--known as the principle of **dependent co-origination** has been groundbreaking towards the development of modern quantum models of matter, and energy (Chapter 5).

Just as there are specific quantum levels of energy for each of the electrons in an atom (**5.5**), there are quantum levels explicit to the energies of the heart's field, consciousness and beyond. Furthermore, just like the atom, each possesses its own unique energy signature. This book has repeatedly braided and returned to the focus of your heart because of the overwhelming anecdotal evidence from all traditions supporting its role as the portal, or conduit, through which divine energies may interface with this physical realm.

According to Carl Jung, the awakened or enlightened self sees the one and all in everything. His work focused on integrating the conscious and unconscious mind to deepen the sense of self. To Jung, the human psyche was by nature religious, seeking to understand the meaning of life and death. This search led to a sense of separation within the soul and he believed that to heal the soul it would require a journey within to meet the self and the divine at the same time. To him, the mandala was an archetype of wholeness, where the self and the divine become one. When you have completed this aspect of your journey, the ability to see through time and space becomes accessible with a single thought.

During heightened states of awareness, a fleeting sense of things at higher frequencies is sometimes experienced. But just like an electron that needs sufficient energy to "jump" from a lower energy level to a higher one, so too the human heart needs to evolve and *fill* specific frequencies. This process is supported through personal reflection, meditation, and cultivating the uplifting awareness facilitated by hope, awe, and compassion. Many saints and ascended masters have shown the way, but there are no shortcuts to the nirvana of emptiness. It may take thousands of lifetimes to harmonize your existence with the multidimensional frequencies of evolved beings such as the Christ or Buddha.

Around the world progressive medical centers are focusing on health and healing in a more caring way that partners medical professionals with patients. This approach focuses on the individual and considers the multidimensional aspects of their being. These innovative programs are leading the way towards a more holistic form of medical care and examples include: Duke Integrative Medicine (Duke University Health System), Stanford Center for Integrative Medicine (Stanford University), Arizona Center for Integrative Medicine (University or Arizona), University of Michigan Integrative Medicine and Harvard Medical School. Such approaches epitomize the following quote:

"Pythagorus said that the most divine art was that of healing.
And if the healing art is the most divine it must occupy
itself with the soul as well as with the body; for no creature
can be sound so long as the higher part in it is sickly."
—Appollonius of Tyana

9.5 Final Thoughts

"The Grateful Heart"

"Wow
Where does the real poetry
Come from?

...From the heart saying,
Shouting,

I am so damn
Alive."

—edited by MJ Ryan

I love to walk the beach at low tide. In the early morning, kelp drapes the shoreline like a green velvet cloak and the sculpted sandstone flashes like giant jewels in the light. Pink and purple starfish cling under their overhangs whilst tiny pools swarming with baby crabs, mussels, and anemones nestle amongst the nooks and crannies. Each microcosm feels vibrant, alive. As the tide turns, the sea covers them once again, returning them to their union with the sea--like a mother cloaking her children in a blanket.

Your heart issues are like the variegated shore--full of nooks and crannies--but all bound by the sea of the Universal Energy Fields. Some are elusive, some are invisible but all are intertwined in ways that are still unfathomable. Moreover, just as the rhythm of the sea chooses to reveal what is or is not to be seen; so do the veils of your heart.

Many years ago I took a fascinating course called Biochemical Adaptations. At that time, the major biochemical pathways had been mapped and were perceived as complete. My professor, Dr. Peter Hochaka thought otherwise. His research focused on organisms capable of living in extreme environments and able to tolerate conditions fatal to most other living things. One of his questions was "How can air breathing mammals such as seals survive under water for 20 min or more without oxygen?" He discovered that in addition to the regular pathways for energy metabolism (**2.7**) the seals had developed an alternative biochemical pathway to be used during extended submersion. Biochemistry became malleable and was no longer seen as an absolute!

Recent discoveries have demonstrated the existence of DNA repair systems within each cell. This means that if a gene is damaged by age, radiation, illness etc., each cell is able to repair its own DNA. When this is considered alongside the impact heart centered thoughts and emotions can have on your wellbeing, who are you to limit yourself to damaged DNA or a broken heart?

Although humans in general, are always ready to embrace a new type of clothing, or car, or way of cooking, the idea of changing the metabolism of your body, your emotions, your thoughts and spirit seems impossible. The evidence shows life is mutable and change is the norm. Nothing is fixed. The universe is within you and is you. You are the **Pratîtya-Samutpâda-âdi!**

GLOSSARY

Acetylcholine: the first neurotransmitter to be identified, it is one of many neurotransmitters associated with the ANS.

Acetyl coenzyme A: conversion of pyruvate to this substance provides entry to the Krebs cycle of aerobic metabolism

Activity Series: a table ranking the ability of metals to resist corrosion due to the relative attraction they have for electrons.

Active transport: a specific means of moving substances across the cell membrane either into or out of the cell.

Adenosine Di-phosphate (ADP): The precursor molecule for ATP, it consists of two phosphate groups attached to an adenosine unit and it is regenerated whenever the third phosphate group is released to provide cellular energy.

Adenosine Tri-phosphate (ATP): commonly known as the energy currency of the cell (and life in general), this molecule consists of three phosphate groups attached to an adenosine unit. It is the attachment of the third group that forms a high-energy bond which stores the energy for use by the cell as needed.

Adrenal gland: a small cone shaped organ situated on top of the kidneys that produces epinephrine and to a lesser degree, norepinephrine when stimulated by the SNS, mineralocorticoids such as Aldosterone, glucocorticoids (cortisone and cortisol), and small amounts of the sex hormones androgen and estrogen.

Adrenaline: British name for epinephrine

Adrenergic receptor: a type of receptor on a target cell that binds to catecholamines such as epinephrine and norepinephrine to produce the "fight or flight" response resulting from sympathetic nervous system stimulation.

Adrenocorticotropic hormone (ACTH): also known as corticotropin is a hormone produced and secreted by the anterior pituitary gland. It is an important messenger amongst the adrenal, hypothalamus and pituitary glands and is often produced in response to stress along with its precursor corticotropin-releasing hormone that is released by the hypothalamus. The principal effect of ACTH is the production of cortisol.

Adverse Childhood Experiences (ACE): traumatic life events that are experienced in childhood

Aerobic: refers to a chemical reaction that takes places in the presence of, or consumes oxygen. At the cellular level, aerobic respiration uses oxygen to obtain chemical energy from glucose (blood sugar) for the manufacture of ATP.

Afferent nerves: carry signals form the muscles and sensory organs to the central nervous system.

Agonists: a substance that a receptor in the cell membrane is designed to bind with so as to open an information channel or gateway into the cell.

Antagonist: a substance that binds with a receptor in the cell membrane and blocks its ability to bind with those substances it is designed to receive.

Aldosterone: a hormone secreted by the adrenal gland which increases the absorption of sodium by the kidneys and thus regulates blood levels of potassium chloride, bicarbonate, blood volume, pH, and blood pressure.

Alternating current: electrical current which alternates travelling in each of 2 directions

Alveoli: tiny thin-walled sacs in the lungs, wherein the exchange of oxygen and carbon dioxide occurs between the body and atmosphere.

Alpha receptor: see Adrenergic receptor

Alpha waves: brain waves generated when you are physically and mentally relaxed and range from 8 to 13 Hz.

Amino acid: a unit used to build peptides and proteins that is identified by the presence of both amino and carboxylic acid functional groups.

Ampere: a unit for measuring the rate of flow of electrical charge.

Amygdala: an almond shaped group of neurons in the brain's limbic system that is associated with the processing of emotions.

Anaerobic: taking place without oxygen or concerning an organism such as yeast that lives in the absence of oxygen.

Aorta: approximately 3 cm in diameter, it is the main trunk of the primary blood vessel leaving the ventricles of the heart and delivering blood from the heart to various parts of the body.

Aortic arch: after it passes upward to form the ascending aorta, the aorta turns turns backwards and to the left at approximately the level of the fourth thoracic vertebra forming the aortic arch. This vessel has three branches and supplies the head, arms and upper thoracic regions.

Arrhythmia: variation from the normal rhythm of the heart.

Artery: a blood vessel that delivers blood from the heart to various body parts.

Atom: the smallest possible particle or unit of matter that retains all the properties of a specific element. Consists of a nucleus with protons and neutrons with orbiting electrons

Atrial natriuretic peptide (ANP): a peptide produced by the atria of the heart involved in the excretion of sodium ions by the kidneys and the regulation of blood volume and pressure

Atomic number: the number of protons in the nucleus of an atom which also determine the chemical and physical properties of an element e.g. atomic number 2 is helium and it has 2 protons in its nucleus

Atrioventricular node (AV-node): a node located near the bottom of the right atrium whose role is to delay the contraction of the ventricles by a 1/10 of a second so that the ventricle can fill from the atrium prior to contracting.

Atrium: an upper chamber of the heart, which receives blood from the body.

Aura: a metaphysical term for the human energy field or bio-field.

Auscultation: listening for sounds in the body especially the chest and abdomen.

Autogenic relaxation: a type of technique such as self-hypnosis used by oneself to induce relaxation.

Autonomic Nervous System (ANS): one of the three main components of the nervous system, its key task is to maintain balance in the body by controlling involuntary activities of body tissues, blood vessels, organs, and glands. The ANS shares some components of the CNS and PNS although it has its own chains of nerve ganglia alongside the spinal cord and in the head.

Axiom: a premise or starting point of reasoning so evident as to be accepted without controversy.

Axon: insulated fiber extending from a nerve cell designed to carry electrical signals

B

Balancing: a term used in energy medicine to describe the realignment of the biofield to its natural, highest frequencies and potentials.

Barometer: device used to detect or measure changes in pressure.

Barometric pressure: the amount of force exerted through pressure.

Barometric wave: a pressure wave working through a medium such as water or air.

Baroreceptors: special nerve cells embedded in the walls of various tissues such as the skin, heart, and blood vessels which detect stretching and changes in pressure.

Battery: two or more electrochemical cells linked together.

Behaviorism: the theory that human and animal behaviour can be explained in terms of conditioning, without appeal to thoughts or feelings, and that psychological disorders are best treated by altering behavior patterns.

Beta-blockers: chemicals which reduce blood pressure by blocking epinephrine.

Betamethasone: a glucocorticoid (synthetic) used to treat many inflammatory conditions such as dermatitis, arthritis, inflammatory bowel disease, reactive airway disease and respiratory distress syndrome in infants.

Beta waves: brain waves generated during active and awake states ranging from 13 to 32 Hz.

Bioelectricity: electrical signals produced by biological organisms.

Bio-electromagnetics: electrical and magnetic signals produced by living organisms.

Bio-field: a scientific term for the energetic emanations that surround and extend beyond the human body; as measured by SQUID (Superconducting Quantum Interference Device) and demonstrated through the mechanism of Kirlian photography.

Biofeedback: a variety of techniques that give the subject information as to how an action or thought affects them.

Biomarkers: substances produced by the body, which may be used to measure the levels of biological function e.g. cortisol levels correlate to experienced levels of stress.

Bio-magnetic: magnetic fields produced by living organisms.

Biophoton: a unit of light produced by a living organism

Blood: a complex fluid circulating throughout the body, which transports nutrients, platelets, blood cells, information, and wastes to their designated locations.

Blood Pressure: the force or push driving the blood through the body.

Brachial artery: main arterial blood vessel supplying one of the arms.

Brain state training: a program designed to improve conscious awareness and control over mental states

Brain natriuretic peptide (BNP): the second polypeptide to be discovered, it is produced when there is increased pressure or stretching of the ventricles of the heart and acts to slow heart rate and lower blood pressure to produce a state of relaxation

Brainstem: a stem like portion of the brain that extends from the spinal cord into the center of brain and acts as a connection between the two. It includes the medulla oblongata, pons, midbrain and forebrain.

Brain waves: electrical patterns produced by the brain during different types of mental activity.

Bronchioles: minute passageways connecting the bronchial tubes of the lungs to the tiny alveolar sacs.

Bundle of HIS: a special bundle of fast-conducting muscle fibers (**Purkinje**): which originate in the AV node and carry the signals for the contraction of the ventricles in the heart

C

Cardiac muscle: specialized muscle fibers found in the heart; which possess intercalated discs at their end to end junctions that increase the efficiency of their electrical impulse transmission.

Calcitriol: active form of Vitamin D that is essential for healthy immune, muscular, and skeletal systems, as well as, the absorption of minerals such as calcium and iron.

Capillary: tiniest of all the blood vessels that form a network amongst all the cell of the body. It is here that gas and nutrient exchange occurs between the cells and the circulatory system

Carbon dioxide (CO_2): a substance produced as a byproduct of cellular respiration and is generally released as a gas from the capillaries in the lungs.

Cardiac muscle: a type of muscle unique to the heart distinguished by the presence of specialized discs (intercalated) at the ends of the muscle fibers to speed up the transmission of electrical signals

Cardiac natriuretic peptide (CNP): a heart peptide with similar properties to ANP and BNP that has also been shown to have anticancer properties

Cardiac output: the quantity of blood pumped by the left ventricle of the heart into the aorta each minute.

Cardiovascular fitness: is the ability of the heart, blood cells and lungs to supply oxygen-rich blood to the working muscle tissues and the ability of the muscles to use oxygen to produce energy for movement

Caritas: Latin in origin, it means love for all and is associated with heartfelt charity and kindness

Carotid artery: one of two (left or right) arteries that carry blood through the neck and into the brain.

Catalyst: a substance that alters the rate in which a chemical reaction can take place by providing a (usually) more efficient route.

Catecholamines: biologically active amines derived from the amino acid tyrosine. The list includes metanephrine, dopamine, epinephrine, and norepinephrine all of which exert significant effects upon metabolic rate, body temperature, smooth muscle, the nervous system and cardiovascular system.

Cellular respiration: a series of biochemical reactions that occur in cells to convert glucose and other nutrients into ATP. Oxygen is required for this process while carbon dioxide, water and energy (in the form of ATP) are the products.

Central Nervous System (CNS): the portion of the nervous system that consists of the brain and spinal cord. The function of the CNS is to analyze sensory input and initiate responses. 12 pairs of nerves branch from the brain and 31 from the spinal cord.

Central tendon: a group of strong, thick tendons that anchor the heart and diaphragm, into the center of the chest and limits their vertical movements.

Centering: the process of focusing one's attention and intention to be fully responsive and present to one's client by setting aside personal issues and expectations of outcome.

Cerebellum: part of the hindbrain in charge of voluntary motor control including speech, balance, and posture.

Cerebral Cortex: located within the cerebrum of the brain, it is responsible for processing information and consists of four lobes.

Cerebrum: largest and uppermost part of the brain containing the cerebral cortex, hippocampus, olfactory bulb, and basal ganglia. It is responsible for many processes such as interpreting sensory information, thinking, learning, memory, emotions and fine motor skills.

Chakra: a Sanskrit word for "spinning wheel" used to describe the vortices of the human energy centers.

Chakra Connection: a full body technique used by energy medicine practitioners of Healing Touch to open and connect the energy flow through the chakra system.

Chemical bond: attractive electrical forces that hold atoms together in order to form chemical substances.

Chemical families: groups of elements that display similar physical and chemical properties. Such elements are usually in the same in vertical columns in the Periodic Table of elements.

Ch'i: (preferred spelling is **Qi** and is pronounced "chee") is a Chinese term for energy or vital life force that flows through the chakras, meridians, and the bio-field also known as *prana, ki* or *spiritus.*

Clearing: Hand movements by the practitioner above the client's biofield that facilitate the release of energy blockage. Synonymous with releasing, letting go, smoothing or unruffling of the biofield,

Chloride (Cl⁻¹): when an atom of chlorine accepts an additional electron it becomes the negatively charged chloride ion.

Coherence: in reference to electromagnetic energy the term refers to having the same wavelength, in common language it also means sticking together, and being logically or aesthetically consistent. It can also refer to the integration of diverse elements or values.

Conductor: any substance that carries the flow or transfer of heat and electricity

Conformation: the characteristic three-dimensional shape assumed by one or more polypeptides especially structural proteins such as microtubules

Cortisol: also called hydrocortisone, a hormone (glucocorticoid) produced by the adrenal gland in response to stress and low blood sugar levels. It is related to cortisone in terms of its physiological effects and plays an important role in increasing blood sugar through gluconeogenesis. It suppresses the immune system and so decreases inflammation but increases the time needed for wound healing. It also aids in the metabolism of fats, proteins and carbohydrates and yet decreases bone and collagen formation.

Cortisone: a hormone (glucocorticoid) produced by the adrenal gland that regulates the metabolism of fats, carbohydrates, sodium, potassium, and proteins. It is also an important anti-inflammatory agent in the body.

Corrosion: the disintegration of a substance (usually a metal) due to loss electrons.

Coulomb: the amount of electrical charge transferred in one second by one ampere of current.

Craniosacral: a complementary therapy designed to balance the energy flow and fluid rhythms between the brain and spinal cord.

Creatine: is produced in the kidney and liver from the amino acids glycine and arginine. It is stored primarily in the brain and skeletal muscle as part of the phosphagen pathway and is used to regenerate phosphocreatine

Creatine phosphate: see phosphocreatine

Curare: a paralytic drug derived from plant resins used by S. American hunters to immobilize their prey. Synthetic versions are used to relax skeletal muscles during anesthesia and critical care.

Cytokines: regulatory proteins, such as lymphokines and interleukins that are produced by the cells and act as mediators of cell to cell communication especially in the control of inflammation and the immune response.

Cytosol: an aqueous, jelly-like fluid that fills and supports the structure of a cell and its organelles.

D

7-Dehydrocholesterol: a substance in your skin that in the presence of sunlight (UVB especially) produces an inactive form of Vitamin D.

Definite proportions: a fixed or constant ratio of atoms which make up a specific substance i.e. water or H_2O consists of two units of hydrogen to one unit of oxygen

Delta waves: longest and slowest brainwaves of the regular EEG measurements ranging from 0.5 to 4 Hz.

7-dehydrocholesterol: substance in the skin that is activated by UV light to produce an inactive form of Vitamin D.

Dehydroepiandrosterone (DHEA): a steroid hormone produced by the adrenal glands, gonads and the brain. It acts as an intermediate in the body's manufacture of sex steroids and is involved with the growth and survival of both developing, and mature neurons

Dendrites: minute fibers extending from nerve cells designed to receive signals

Deoxyribonucleic acid (DNA): an extremely large biological molecule that carries the genetic code or blueprint of life for an organism.

Dependent Co-origination: Buddhist premise that everything is related to everything else hence the existence of all things is dependent upon the existence of everything else.

Depolarization: in higher organisms the cells maintain an internal environment that is negatively charged relative to the cell's exterior known as the membrane potential during depolarization, the negative internal charge of the cell temporarily becomes more positive.

Direct current (DC): electrical charge travelling in one direction only

Diuresis: increased need to urinate usually caused by increased urine output from the kidneys

Dopamine: an important neurotransmitter produced in the brain used to regulate behavior related to rewards and motivation, motor control and the release of hormones such as prolactin and gonadotropin releasing hormone.

Double slit experiments: originally conducted by Thomas Young, they were pivotal in demonstrating the dual nature of light i.e. it exhibits both wave and particle properties

Dualism: as condition or situation consisting of two opposing or contrasting aspects.

E

Efferent nerves: carry signals from the central nervous system to the muscles and sensory organs.

Electrocardiogram (ECG): the record produced when electrodes are placed on the surface of the body on opposite sides of the heart, in order to follow the changes in electric potential during the contraction of heart muscle.

Electric Current: the rate of flow of charge past a point in an electric circuit.

Electric Field: a region around a charged particle or object within which a force would be exerted on other charged particles or objects.

Electric Field Strength: a numerical measurement of the intensity of an electric field or force per charge. Newtons (force) per Coulombs (charge) or N/C is the commonly used expression.

Electric Potential: occurs when a difference in electrical charges builds up between 2 or more situations.

Electrochemical Cell: a device capable of generating an electrical potential from a chemical reaction or facilitating it.

Electron: a small negatively charged sub-atomic particle

Electroencephalogram (EEG): the record produced when electrodes are placed on the scalp or brain in order to track changes in the electric potential of various areas of the brain.

Electrolyte: a substance—usually an ionic compound or "salt" that dissolves in water (and other solvents) to form solutions that conduct electricity e.g. table salt dissolves in water to release the Na^{+1} and Cl^{-1} ions which make the solution a good conductor of electric charge.

Electrolytic conduction: the transfer of an electrical charge by the net movement of positively and negatively charged ions (in solution) to poles of opposite electrical charge.

Electromagnetic field: a region of space created by electromagnetic energy.

Electromagnetic force: the second strongest of the four forces of nature. It acts between particles with electric charges.

Electromagnetic (EM) spectrum: a chart used to organize the range of wavelengths and frequencies of electromagnetic energy (light) energy.

Electronegativity: the force of attraction an atom or ion has for electrons.

Electron: a small negatively charged sub-atomic particle that has a specific energy within an atom and is responsible for the chemical properties of the elements.

Electrophysiology: the branch of physiology that pertains to the flow of ions (ion current) in biological tissues and the electrical recording techniques that enable the measurement of this flow.

Electron Transport Chain: a biochemical reaction that is a crucial part of aerobic respiration. Electrons are basically passed along the membrane of the mitochondria and accepted by oxygen to produce water.

Element: a pure substance containing only one type of atom.

ELF: the longest waves in the electromagnetic spectrum with a wavelength of 100,000 m to 10,000 km

Energy Field: a region or area produced by various types of energy e.g. electrical, magnetic, gravitational etc.

Endocrine: substances (hormones) produced by various organs in the body used to regulate physiology e.g. liver, pancreas, thyroid etc.

Endocrinology: study of the hormones, peptides and organs involved in regulating growth, repair, and maintenance of the body.

Endorphins: powerful substances produced by the body which generate strong sense of well-being and reduce perception of pain.

Endoplasmic reticulum: an organelle found in the cell that looks like a network of tubular membranes involved in the synthesis of cell products.

Entanglement: in quantum theory, a term used to describe the manner in which particles such as photons, electrons or quibits that have interacted with each other retain a connection through time and space.

Entrainment: the synchronization of two or more individuals into the same

Enzymes: a biological catalyst i.e. a metabolic molecule; which speeds up a chemical reaction.

Epinephrine: produced by the adrenal glands upon stimulation of the sympathetic nervous system. Classed as a catecholamine, it produces a global physiological reaction to stress that includes: increases in blood pressure and cardiac output, dilation of respiratory airways, and increased blood sugar (glucose). These effects make it a key agent in treating cardiac life support, systemic allergic reactions, restricted airways and hemorrhage.

Ethics: study of morality's effect on a person's conduct.

Ethnographic: study of an ethnic or cultural group.

Eudaimonia: an ancient Greek ideology based on the belief that all humans can thrive by encouraging the infusion of good spirits.

F

Fatty acid: a basic unit of fats composed of a carbon and hydrogen chain with a carboxylic acid group at one end of the chain.

Fermentation: a metabolic process that occurs naturally in yeast, bacteria and muscles involving the conversion of sugars to either acids or alcohol.

Fetus: a developing organism contained within its mother.

Field: with respect to an electric charge, its force extends outward and permeates all of the space around it which is known as its field.

Frequency: the number of wave crests that pass a fixed point in a second.

Functional groups: specific groups of atoms or bonds within molecules responsible for characteristic chemical properties.

Functional Magnetic Resonance Imaging (fMRI): measures brain activity by detecting changes associated with blood flow based on the coupling of cerebral blood flow and neuronal activation.

G

GABA (gamma amino butyric acid): a inhibitory neurotransmitter that helps neurons recover after firing and has a sedative effect. It is involved in the regulation of norepinephrine, epinephrine, dopamine and serotonin.

Galvanization: a process of coating iron and other metals in zinc to resist corrosion.

Gamma waves: the shortest and fastest of the brainwaves ranging from 32 to 100 Hz.

Gauss: a unit for measuring the density of a magnetic field such that one gauss is equal to one maxwell per square centimeter--10,000 gauss equals one Tesla.

Glycine: a non-essential amino acid.

Glycolysis: a nearly universal sequence of reactions that converts glucose to pyruvate and produces ATP

Glucose: a simple sugar composed of a chain of six carbon, twelve hydrogen and six oxygen atoms.

Gluconeogeneisis: a metabolic process that produces glucose from non-carbohydrate sources such as pyruvate and lactate.

Golgi apparatus: a cell organelle involved in the packaging and storage of cell products.

Gravity: the force of attraction between two or more objects related to their relative masses.

H

Harmonic analysis: a branch of mathematics concerned with the representation of functions or signals as the superposition of basic waves, and the study of and generalization of the notions of Fourier series and Fourier transforms.

Harmonious: concordant, forming a consistent or agreeable whole; free from dissent; sweet sounding; singing, playing tunefully.

Harmonize: Bring into, be in Harmony (with) make, be agreeable in artistic effect; add notes to (melody) to form chords.

Harmony: Agreement; agreeable effect of arrangement of parts; combination of simultaneous notes to form chords (of Melody); sweet or melodious sound; collation of parallel narratives etc., esp of the four gospels.

Healing Touch: a complementary bio-field therapy with an emphasis on restoring balance and harmony to the human energy field and bodies.

Heart Rate Variability (HRV): variation in the time interval between heartbeats as measured from the beat-to-beat interval.

Heisenberg Uncertainty Principle: a law used in quantum theory stating that certain pairs of physical properties such as momentum and position cannot be precisely known at the same time.

Hemorrhage: large loss of blood through accident, injury, or illness.

Hemoglobin: the iron containing pigment found in red blood cells that carries oxygen from the lungs to the tissues and cells.

Heroin: also known as, diamorphine is a synthetic opoid drug produced by reacting morphine with acetic anhydride.

Hertz (Hz): the unit used to represent frequency i.e. the number of wave crests or cycles that pass a fixed point in a second.

Hormone: a substance secreted by an organ, gland or body part that is conveyed through the blood stream to another body part and chemically stimulates that part to either increase or decrease its secretion of another hormone.

Human energy field (HEF): subtle, structured fields of energy produced by the human body also referred to as biofields and the aura.

Hydronium ion: a water molecule that is bonded to a proton (H$^+$). This forms an H$_3$O$^+$ ion.

Hypertrophy: enlargement or overgrowth of an organ or part due to increase in size of its constituent cells e.g. ventricular hypertrophy is an example of an enlarged ventricle in the heart.

Hypertension: a condition in which blood pressure is consistently higher than 140 mm Hg systolic or 90 mm Hg diastolic

Hypoglossal nerve: a nerve that connects the pharynx to the back of the tongue and provides access to the brainstem and vagus nerve.

Hypothalamus: located in the brain between the pituitary and thalamus, this structure works with the pituitary to regulate hormones.

I

Immunology: a branch of science focused on the structure and function of the immune system, its roles in immune responses, and autoimmune disorders,

Induction: a process wherein either electricity or magnetism is passed between two objects or circuits without physical contact

Inert Gas: a substance that generally does not undergo chemical reactions, also called the noble gases Neon is an example of this chemical family

Infrared: usually associated with heat, these frequencies of the electromagnetic spectrum are slower than visible light and range between 1 mm and 750 nm.

Insulator: a substance that does not conduct heat or electricity

Intercostal muscles: inter means "between" and "costal" refers to the ribs hence these muscles are found between the ribs and are responsible for the movement of the chest.

Interleukin-6: a molecule used as a biomarker for inflammation. Higher levels correlate to greater inflammation and vice versa.

Ion: an electrically charged species composed of one or more types of atoms.

Ionic Bond: a bond formed by the electrical attraction of two oppositely charged ions

Ionosphere: an outer layer of the earth's rich in ions and electrons extending 80 to 1,000 km beyond the surface of the earth.

Ionizing Radiation: radiation that is capable of breaking chemical bonds and penetrating matter such as X-rays and gamma rays.

Ischemic Heart Disease: restricted blood flow to the heart most often the result of plaque deposits that harden the arteries.

J

K

Kinetic energy: the relative movement or vibration of particles in a substance. When a substance is exposed to infrared (heat) energy it's particles exhibit an increase in kinetic energy.

Kirlian photography: a process in which a high-frequency electric field is applied to an object so that it radiates a pattern of luminescence (or aura) that is recorded on photographic film.

Krebs cycle: an aerobic pathway for the production of ATP found in the mitochondria of the cell.

Kwashiorkor: a metabolic condition brought on by insufficient calorie intake especially proteins, in the diet. It is characterized by impaired intestinal and liver function, poor immunity, anemia and edema to name a few and is frequently fatal especially in infants and young children.

L

Lactic acid: a three carbon molecule formed from pyruvate during the last phase of anaerobic activity, it dissociates to form lactate.

Larynx: also known as the voice box, it is responsible for the control of air flow during speech.

Left Atrium: the third chamber of the heart; which receives oxygenated blood from the lungs and pumps it into the left ventricle.

Left Inferior Parietal Lobe (IPL): a region of the brain associated with the ability to understand numbers, manipulate objects and perform writing tasks

Left Ventricle: the fourth chamber of the heart; which receives blood from the left atrium and pumps out to the body.

Light: electromagnetic radiation that can propagates through empty space with an electrical field in the vertical plane and a magnetic field in the horizontal plane

Limbic system: a part of the brain associated with emotional control it is found on each side of the thalamus and just below the cerebrum

M

Magnetic Field: a vector field created by magnetized material or moving electric charges both its strength and direction varies with its location.

Magnetite: a darkish shiny mineral of iron oxide (Fe_3O_4) known for its magnetic properties.

Medulla oblongata: a continuation of the spinal cord within the skull, containing control centers for the heart and lungs and forming the lowest part of the brainstem.

Metabolism: the chemical processes occurring within a living cell or organism that are necessary for the maintenance of life

Metabolic pathway: a series of steps found in biochemical reactions that help convert molecules or substrates, such as sugar, into different, more readily usable substances to support the needs of a living organism.

Metal: elements found on the left side of the periodic table that exhibit common properties including a shiny luster and the ability to conduct heat and electricity.

Metallic conduction: the outer electrons of metals are considered to be somewhat loosely associated and, as a consequence, capable of flowing or moving through a metal when an external electrical charge is applied and thus conduct an electrical current.

Metalloids: an element whose properties are a mixture of metals and nonmetals.

Metanephrine: an inactive metabolite of epinephrine.

Microtubules: minute networks of connective tissue that provide structural support and information transfer inside a cell

Microwaves: part of the electromagnetic spectrum with wavelengths ranging from 187-10 mm.

Mitochondria:

Mindfulness: the practice of being fully present and aware in the moment without being over reactive or emotional.

Mineralocorticoids: hormones released by the adrenal gland that control the levels of minerals such as calcium and potassium in the body and hence affect fluid retention, electrolytes and blood pressure e.g. Aldsosterone.

Mitochondria: tiny structures or organelles found within cells that are responsible for cellular respiration and leads to the production of ATP—the energy currency of life.

Modulation: the process of adding information to a steady waveform such as an electronic or optical carrier signal. This term is usually applied to electromagnetic signals.

Molecule: a substance formed from one or more types of atoms generally held together by the sharing of electrons i.e. covalent bonds.

Myelin sheath: A complex membrane primarily composed of lipids, proteins, and water that surrounds the axon of a neuron and acts to insulate it during conduction of electrical signals.

N

Naloxone: (sold as **narcan**), is a key component of drug overdose kits and works by reversing the depression of the central nervous system and respiratory system caused by opioids. It is known as an opoid antagonist.

Nanometer (nm): a unit of measurement in the metric system wherein 1 nm equals 10^{-9} meters.

Natriuresis: means to "make water" and refers to the increased excretion of sodium ions (Na^+) in the urine via the kidneys, which lowers the concentration of sodium in the blood and also lowers blood volume.

Natriuretic: a drug that increases the rate in which sodium ions are excreted in the urine.

Negatively charged ion: when an atom or species acquires an excess of electrons compared to the number of protons it is designated as having a negative electrical charge.

Neurology: an area of medicine dealing with the diagnosis and treatment of the central and peripheral nervous systems as well as their associated tissues and organs such as the muscles of the skeletal system and digestive system.

Neurofeedback: a type of biofeedback used to help the individual train their brainwaves.

Neuromelanin: a dark pigment found in the brain; which is structurally related to melanin.

Neurotransmitter: a substance used for direct signaling between the neurons of the brain and body Usually, released when the axon of a pre-synaptic neuron is excited, it acts by inhibiting or exciting a target cell examples of common neurotransmitters include: acetylcholine, dopamine, norepinephrine, and serotonin.

Neutron: a tiny sub-atomic particle with no electrical charge

Norepinephrine: a substance that acts as a neurotransmitter when released by neurons or as a hormone when produced by the adrenal gland. It is able to constrict blood vessels without affecting the output of the heart. Therapeutically, it is used to manage severe hypotension induced by neurogenic or septic shock.

Nervous System: one of the regulatory systems of the body designed to transmit electrochemical impulses. It consists of millions of neurons and includes the central, peripheral and autonomic nervous systems along with their supporting cells and structures.

Neutron: a subatomic particle mostly found in the nucleus of an atom that does not carry an electric charge—hence it is neutral.

Node: In the heart it is a specialized type of tissue that contracts like a muscle but also releases an electrical message like a nerve.

Nonmetal: an element that does not display the properties of a metal. This may include one or more of the following: insulator, brittle, dull, gaseous at room temperature, forms negative ions or is inert

Nucleus: the small central region of the atom which contains most of the mass and all of the positive charge

Nuclear Fusion: a reaction in which the nucleus of two or more atoms fuse to form a new nucleus of one or more different atoms. Any change in mass is manifested by a huge release of energy

O

Occipital ridge: a bony ridge at the back of the head where the base of the skull meets the spine.

Ohm: the unit for electrical resistance

Opoid antagonist: any substance that blocks opoid receptors in the body

Oxide (O^{-2}): when an atom of oxygen accepts two additional electrons it becomes an ion with a -2 charge

Oxytocin: a polypeptide hormone, produced by the posterior lobe of the pituitary gland that stimulates contraction of the smooth muscle of the uterus, milk let-down, and is associated with bonding and attachment.

P

P wave: a portion of the ECG corresponding to the contraction of the atria and the subsequent depolarization of the nerves and muscles

Pacemaker: see Sino-Atrial Node

Paracrine: secretion of a hormone from a source other than an endocrine gland. When this occurs in a tissue, secretions by one cell type influence the activity of neighboring cells and this is known as paracrine control.

PEMS: an acronym for the physical, emotional, mental and spiritual energy bodies of the human energy system.

Peptides: a substance consisting of two or more amino acids linked in a chain, the carboxyl group of each acid being joined to the amino group of the next.

Peptide bond: a covalent bond formed by joining the carboxyl group of one amino acid to the amino group of another, with the removal of a molecule of water.

Permissive: giving permission or allowing

Peripheral Circulatory System: consists of the veins and arteries not in the chest or abdomen (i.e. in the arms, hands, legs and feet) and the arterial system supplies oxygenated blood to the body, while the peripheral veins lead deoxygenated blood from the capillaries in the extremities back to the heart.

Peripheral Nervous system: 43 pairs of nerves from the brain and spinal cord that form a network throughout the body, sends sensory data to the central nervous system (CNS), and carries response messages to the body.

pH: an abbreviation for the negative log of the hydronium ion concentration in moles per liter. Acidic solutions are considered to have a low pH value while basic solutions have a high number.

Phosphocreatine (PCr): also known as creatine phosphate is a molecule that is synthesized in the liver and transported through the blood to the muscles for storage where it serves as a reserve of energy in the form of high energy phosphate bonds that can be used in an instant.

Phosphagen: a biochemical pathway that uses creatine phosphate for the rapid production of energy when the muscles must respond instantly to a demand.

Photochemical reaction: a chemical reaction that requires light in order for it to proceed. Photosynthesis in plants and the human body's ability to manufacture vitamin D are examples of such reactions.

Photoelectric effect: the act of shining a light on the surface of a metal, causes a metal to become positively charged as the energy provided by the light causes electrons to escape from the formerly neutral metal atoms.

Photon: the fundamental particle of light (quantum) that carries electromagnetic energy.

Pituitary gland: a pea sized gland in the center of the skull behind the bridge of the nose which links the nervous and endocrine systems and releases many hormones affecting growth, sexual development, metabolism and more

Pons: an area of the hindbrain that lies directly above the medulla it is involved in communication amongst different regions of the brain, is associated with the regulation of breathing, sleep, and the senses, as well as facial expressions

Polypeptides: chains consisting of more than one hundered amino acids

Positively charged ion: when an atom or species has a deficit of electrons compared to protons it is assigned a positive electrical charge.

Post traumatic stress disorder (PTSD): a mental health condition triggered by a terrifying event — either experiencing it or witnessing it. Symptoms may include flashbacks, nightmares and severe anxiety, as well as uncontrollable thoughts about the event.

Proton: small positively charged sub-atomic particle

Pranayama: commonly broken down into two roots *prana*, meaning life or breath energy and *yama,* meaning restraint or control. When the second root becomes *ayama,* it means *un*restrains the breath and hence honors those aspects of breath not under voluntary control as well as, those that are.

Pratîtya-Samutpáda-ádi: Buddhist principle of wholeness described as *everything* and *nothing* which is represented by an Empty Circle.

Pre-ganglionic: situated in front of, or prior to a mass of nerve cell bodies or tissue

Proton: a subatomic particle with a positive charge that is mostly found in the nucleus.

Psychoendoneuroimmunology (PENI): a paradigm that provides the concepts and mechanisms for studying and explaining mind-body relationships. It incorporates ideas, belief systems, hopes, and desires as well as biochemistry, physiology, and anatomy. It operates on the principle that as we change our thoughts, we change our brain, our biology, and our body.

Psychosomatic: refers to the effects of the mind and emotions upon the body

Pulmonary artery: the major blood vessel leaving the right ventricle of the heart and transporting blood to the lungs for oxygenation and waste removal.

Pulmonary vein: major blood vessel enriched with oxygen and carries blood to the left atrium of the heart.

Purkinje fiber: a special type of cardiac muscle that transmits electrical impulses about 6 times faster than cardiac muscle.

Pulsed Electromagnetic Field (PEMF) Therapy: a medical device that induces small electrical currents to flow in the tissues it is directed towards e.g. bone, ligaments, nerves etc.

Pyruvate: a molecule formed during glycolysis containing 3 carbon atoms.

Q

Quanta: a package or unit that is separate or discrete

Quantum: plural of quanta.

QRS complex: a region of the ECG corresponding to the sequence of depolarization as the ventricles contract

R

Radial artery: a continuation of the brachial artery that travels down the radial side of the forearm to the wrist.

Radio waves: part of the electromagnetic spectrum and longer than microwaves radio waves range from 0.187 m to 600 m.

Receptor: 1) an organ or cell able to respond to an external stimulus such as heat or light and transmit a signal to a sensory nerve e.g. the cells in the retina of the eye send signals to the brain via the optic nerve. 2) a protein molecule or structure inside or on the surface of a cell that receives and binds with hormones, antigens, drugs and neurotransmitters that cause a change in the activity of that particular cell e.g. epinephrine binds to receptors in smooth muscle causing it to contract

Red Blood Cells (erythrocytes): contain a transport protein called hemoglobin designed to deliver oxygen to the body tissues—via blood flow through the circulatory system.

Reflex arc: a nerve pathway in the body that connects certain muscle groups to others, without involving the brain and usually result in involuntary responses.

Remote viewing: the practice of seeking impressions about a distant or unseen target using extrasensory perception.

Resistance: the degree to which a substance opposes or inhibits the flow of an electric current.

Resonance: in physics, it is a phenomenon in which an external force or a vibrating system forces another system to vibrate with greater amplitude at specific frequencies.

Right Atrium: the first chamber of the heart that collects the venous blood and lymphatic fluid as it returns from the body.

Right Inferior Parietal Lobe (RPL): a region of the brain associated with the interpretation of spatial information and the regulation of personality

Right Ventricle: the second chamber of the heart; which receives blood from the right atrium and pumps it out towards the lungs

Rough endoplasmic reticulum: a granular membrane in the cell involved in the manufacture of cell products

S

Sciatic nerve: a long nerve found in most vertebrates extending from the 5th lumbar vertebrae through the pelvis and down the outside of the leg to the foot.

Seasonal Affective Disorder (SAD): a type of depression that is related to the seasons. Generally starting in the fall and continuing until spring, treatment may include light therapy, counseling and medications.

Serotonin: an inhibitory neurotransmitter produced primarily by the brain and gut. It is involved in many biological processes and related general wellbeing, self-worth and happiness.

Self-Chakra Connection: a technique taught by Healing Touch Program™ as a form of self-care to restore balance and harmony to the subtle energy systems of the body and promote relaxation.

Sino-atrial node: a small strip of specialized muscle richly enmeshed with nerves which is located in the posterior of the right atrium just below the junction of the superior vena cava and the right atrium

Skeletal muscle: also known as striated muscle, is found in all muscles associated with voluntary or conscious control. The cytoplasm of these cells is distinguished by the presence of bundled myofibrils; which are the basic units of muscle contraction.

Smooth muscle: muscles of the internal organs and tissues such as the digestive system which are under involuntary control and characterized by a spindle shape with a central nucleus.

Soma: means body

Somatic Nervous System (SoNS): is part of the peripheral nervous system and has connections to the skin, muscles, and sensory organs. This system enables voluntary control of skeletal muscles, movement of the body, and reception of sensory input such as light, sound, etc.

Sound: vibrations that travel through the air or another medium and can be heard when they reach a person's ear.

Spiral: coiled: winding continually from a center, whether remaining in the same plane like a watch-spring or rising in a cone.

Spectroscopy: the study of the interaction between matter and electromagnetic radiation

Sternum: the breastbone

Striated muscles: also known as skeletal muscles, they are responsible for the contraction of those voluntary muscles involved in physical movement of the body.

String theory: a theory of physics in which particles are described as patterns of vibration that have length but no height or width—like infinitely thin pieces of string.

Stroke: sudden death of brain cells due to lack of oxygen, usually caused by blockage of blood flow or rupture of an artery to the brain.

Stethoscope: an acoustic medical device for listening to the internal sounds of a body.

Substantia nigra: a layer of deeply pigmented gray matter situated in the midbrain which contains a tract of dopamine-producing nerve cells whose secretion tends to be deficient in conditions such as Parkinson's disease.

Suprasternal notch: a visible dip between the collarbones at the top of the breast bone.

Sympathetic nervous system (SNS): part of the autonomic nervous system whose pre-ganglionic fibers originate in the thoracic and lumbar regions of the spinal cord. This system produces a generalized response designed to prepare the body for stressful situations.

Synapse: a minute gap between two nerve cells, across which impulses pass by diffusion of a neurotransmitter.

T

T wave: a repolarization wave in the ECG which represents the recovery of the ventricles from their contraction

Takotsubo cardiomyopathy: also known as *broken heart syndrome* is a condition caused by a weakening of the left ventricle of the heart that is brought on after severe emotional or physical stress. The main symptoms are chest pain and shortness of breath.

Tempomandibular joint (TMJ): the joint where the jaw or mandible connects with the temporal bone of the skull.

Tesla (T): a unit of magnetic field strength or magnetic flux density.

Thalamus: a limbic system structure in the brain involved in sensory perception and relaying sensory information to the cerebral cortex.

Theta waves: brainwaves that predominate when you are meditating or daydreaming and range from 4 to 8 Hz.

Thorax: the part of the body between the neck and abdomen; it is separated from the abdomen by the diaphragm

Tidal Volume: the volume of air exchanged by the lungs during a cycle of inhalation and exhalation. Average male is 0.5 liters.

Tyrosine: an essential amino acid, chiefly found in corn; used by the body in the manufacture of catecholamines i.e. epinephrine, norepinephrine, and dopamine.

U

Ultraviolet Light: frequencies of light in the electromagnetic spectrum ranging from 10 nm to 400 nm. Ultraviolet light has more energy and shorter wavelengths than visible light.

UVB: a portion of electromagnetic energy in the ultraviolet range with frequencies of 280 to 315 nm

V

Vagal tone: refers to the level of activity of the vagus nerve; good tone is related to how easily one is able to relax and is associated with good health

Vagus nerve: the 10th cranial nerve; it runs from the brain through the face to the thorax and abdomen and is involved in regulation of heart rate, respiration and other autonomic functions

Vasorelaxation: relaxation of the smooth muscles lining the blood vessels that usually results in decreased blood pressure

Vein: a blood vessel that carries blood from the body to the heart.

Vena Cava: the superior vena cava is the large vein which returns blood to the heart from the head, neck and upper limbs while the inferior vena cava returns blood to the heart from the rest of the body.

Ventricular natriuretic peptide (VNP): a peptide produced by the ventricles of the heart involved in the secretion of sodium ions by the kidneys and the maintenance of blood volume and pressure.

Venous return: the quantity of blood flowing from the veins into the right atrium of the heart each minute.

Ventricle (heart): one of two large chambers in the heart that collect and expel blood from an atrium towards the peripheral beds within the body.

Vibration: when an initial force causes movement that spreads outward in a wave and carries the energy from one place to the next. In a medium like air or water, the particles jostle one another and transfer the energy from particle to particle.

Vitalism: an ancient belief system wherein all living things possess a mysterious vital force

Vitamin D: see **calcitriol**

Voltage (v): the amount of push or pressure forcing electricity through a system

Voltaic pile: an alternating stack of two different metals designed to produce an electric charge travelling in one direction.

Volts: the push or pressure that drives an electric current.

W

Wave-particle duality: is the concept in quantum mechanics that every particle may be partly described in terms not only of particles, but also of waves.

Wavelength: distance between corresponding points of two consecutive waves.

Wavicle: a term to describe the dual—both wave and particle--nature of matter

X

Xyphoid: a bony protrusion that marks the bottom of the sternum

BIBLIOGRAPHY

Ai, A.L, Peterson, C., Gilliespie, B., Boiling, S.F., Jessup, M.G., Behling, B.A. & Pierce, F. (2001). Designing clinical trials on energy healing: ancient art encounters medical science. *Alternative Therapies in Health and Medicine,* 7(4), 83-90.

Alabdulgader, A. (2012). Coherence: A novel non pharmacological modality for lowering blood pressure in hypertensive patients. *Glob. Adv. Health Med, 1(2), 56-64.* doi: 10.7453/gahmi.2012.1.2.011

Barron, B. (1999). Opioid peptides and the heart. *Cardiovascular Research,* 43(1), 13-16. doi:10.1016/s0008-663(99)00112-1

Bailey, A. (1970 a). *A treatise on white magic.* New York, NY: Lucis Publishing Company.

Bailey, A. (1998 b). *Esoteric healing.* New York, NY: Lucis Publishing Company

Baldwin, W. J. (2005). *Spirit releasement therapy.* Terra Alta, WV: Headline Books and Co.

Barker, E. (2017). *New neuroscience reveals four rituals that will make you happy.* Retrieved from https://www.the ladders.com/p/21219/neuroscience-4-rituals-happy.

Beattie, M. (2010). *Journey to the heart: daily meditations on the path to freeing your soul.* HarperSanFrancisco.

Becker, R.O., Seldon, G. (1985). *The body electric: electromagnetism and the foundation of life.* William Morrow, New York.

Bergen-Cico, D., Lane, S., Thompson, M., Wozny, S., Zajdel, M., Noce, J., (2015). The impact of post-traumatic stress on first responders: analysis of cortisol, anxiety, depression, sleep impairment and pain. *International Paramedic Practice* 5(3). Retrieved from https://www.researchgate.net/profile/

Dessa_Bergen-Cico/publication/288021313.The_impact_of_post-traumatic_stress_on_first_responders_analysis_of_ cortisol_ anxiety_depression_sleep_impairment_and_pain/links/56b31b7e08 ae56d7b06d0b67.pdf

Bilsker, D., White, J. (2011). The silent epidemic of male suicide. *British Columbia Medical Journal* 53: 529-534

Boutron, I., Moher, D., Altman, D.G., Schulz, K.F., Ravaud, P. (2008). Extending the CONSORT statement to randomized trials of nonpharmacologic treatment: explanation and elaboration. *Annals of Internal Medicine, 148,* 298-309.

Braden, G. (2007). *The divine matrix: bridging time, space, miracles and belief.* Carlsbad, CA: Hay House.

Brennan, B. (1987a). *Hands of light: a guide to healing through the human energy field.* New York, NY: Bantam Books.

Brennan, B. (1993b). *Light emerging: the journey of personal healing.* New York, NY: Bantam Books.

Brower, V. (2006). Mind-body research moves towards the mainstream. *EMBO Reports* 7(4):358-361. doi: 10.1038/si.embro.7400671

Bruyere, R. (1993). *Wheels of light.* Arcadia, CA: Bon Productions.

Burr, H. (1972). *Blueprint for immortality: the electric patterns of life.* London, England: Spearman.

Capra, F. (1975 a). *The tao of physics.* Boston, MA: Shambala.

Capra, F. (1996 b). *The web of life.* New York, NY: Doubleday.

Childre, D., Martin, H. (2000). *The heartmath solution.* New York, NY: Harper Collins.

Chilton, P. J. (2012). *The heart-mind matrix: how the heart can teach the mind new ways to think.* South Paris, ME: Park Street Press.

Chopra, D. (1989). *Quantum healing: exploring the frontiers of mind/body medicine.* Toronto, ON: Bantam Books.

Clerico, A.,Giannoni, A., Vittorini, S., Passino, C. (2011). Thirty years of the heart as an endocrine organ: physiological role and clinical utility of cardiac natriuretic hormones. *Am J Physiol Heart Circ Physiol,* 301, H12-H20. doi:10.1152/ajpheart00226.2011.

Cook, C. A., Guerrerio, J. F., & Slater, V. E. (2004). Healing touch and quality of life in women receiving radiation treatment for cancer:

a randomized controlled trial. *Alternative Therapies in Health and Medicine, 10*(3), 34-41.

Covey, S. (1989). *The seven habits of highly effective people.* New York, NY: Simon and Schuster.

Cowart, K. (2016). *How constantly complaining will rewire your brain to stay negative.* Retrieved from http://thespiritscience.net/2016/06/25/how-constantly-complaining-will-rewire-your-brain-to-stay-negative/

Cressell, D. (2008). Mindfulness meditation training effects on CD4+T lymphocytes in HIV-1 infected adults: a small randomized controlled trial. *Brain Behav Immun., 23*(2), 184-188. doi: 10.1016/j.bbi.2008.07.004

Dalayeun, J., Nores, J., Bergal, S. (1993). Physiology of beta-endorphins: a close-up view and review of the literature. *Biomed Pharmacother, 47*(8): 311-320.

Dale, C. (2009). *The subtle body: an encyclopedia of your energetic anatomy.* Boulder CO: Sounds True Inc.

De Bold, A. J., Borenstein, H. B., Veress, A.T., Sonnenberg, H. A. (1981). Rapid and important natriuretic response to intravenous injection of atrial myocardial extracts in rats. *Life Sci* 28: 89–94.

Driver, R. (1987). Changing conceptions. *International Seminar on Adolescent Development and School Science.* London, UK: King's College.

Einthoven,W. (1925). *The string galvanometer and the measurement of the action currents of the heart.* Retrieved from http://www.nobelprize.org/nobel_prizes/medicine/laureates/1924/einthoven-lecture.pdf

Finger, A. (2005). *Chakra yoga: balancing energy for physical, spiritual and mental well-being.* Boston, MA: Shamballa Publications.

Fraser, P., & Massey, H. (2008). *Decoding the human body-field: the new science of information as medicine.* Rochester, VT: Healing Arts Press.

Friedman, M. (2017). *History and Overview of PTSD.* Retrieved from https://www.ptsd.va.gov/professional/PTSD-overview/ptsd-overview.asp

Forgues, E. (2009). Methodological issues pertaining to the evaluation of the effectiveness of energy-based therapies: avenues for a methodological guide. *Journal of Complementary and Integrative Medicine,* 6(1), 13, 1-13.

Foundation for Inner Peace (2007). *A course in miracles: combined volume.* Mill Valley, CA: Foundation for Inner Peace.

Frankl, V. (1984). *Man's search for meaning.* New York, NY: Washington Square Press.

Gardner, Howard (1991). *Intelligence reframed: multiple intelligences for the 21ˢᵗ century.* New York, NY: Basic Books.

Gerber, R. (2001). *Vibrational medicine.* Vermont: Bear and Company.

Giancoli, D. (1998). *Physics.* Toronto, ON: Prentice Hall Canada Inc.

Gibson, M. (2012). *The human body of light.* High Point, NC: Tybro Publications.

Ginsberg, J., Berry, M., & Powell, D. (2010). Cardiac coherence and PTSD in combat veterans. *Altern. Ther. Health Med, 16, 52-60.*

Greene, B. (2004). *The fabric of the cosmos.* New York, NY: Vintage Books.

Grey, A. (1990). *Sacred mirrors: the visonary art of Alex Grey.* Rochester, Vermont: Inner Transitions International.

Grippo, A., Trahanas, D., Zimmerman, R., Porges, S., Carter, S. (2009). Oxytocin protects against negative behavioral and autonomic consequences of long-term social isolation. *Psychoneuroendocrinology, 34(10), 1542-1553. doi: 10.1016/j.psyneuen.2009.05.017*

Guarneri, M. (2006). *The Heart Speaks: A Cardiologist Reveals the Secret Language of Healing.* New York, NY: Touchstone

Gutkowska, J., Jankowski, M., Mukaddam-Daher S., & McCann, S. (2000). Oxytocin is a cardiovascular hormone. *Braz. J. Med. Biol. Res., 33(6), 625-633.*

Guyton, A. (1971). *Textbook of medical physiology 4ᵗʰ Ed.* Toronto, ON: W.B. Saunders Company.

Hammerschlag, R., Levin, M., McCraty, R., Bat, N., Ives, J., Lutgendorf, S., Oschman, J. (2015). Biofield physiology: a framework for an emerging discipline

Hansen, R. (2007). *Relaxed and contented: activating the parasympathetic wing of your nervous system.* http://www.wisebrain.org/ParasympatheticNS.pdf.

Hardt, J. (2007). *The art of smart thinking*. Santa Clara, CA: Biocybernaunt Press.

Hardwick, M. E., Pulido, P. A., & Adelson, W. S. (2012). Nursing intervention using healing touch in bilateral total knee arthroplasty. *Orthopaedic Nursing*, 31(1), 5-11.

Hardy, C. (2011). *The sacred network: megaliths, ley lines, and the power of shared consciousness*. Rochester, VT: Inner Traditions.

Hay, L. (2004). *Heal your Body*. Carlsbad, CA: Hay House, Inc.

Healing Touch Program. (2009). *Level 1 notebook (6ᵗʰ ed.)*. San Antonio, TX: author

Healing Touch Program. (2017). *Level 2 notebook (8ᵗʰ ed)*. San Antonio, TX: author

Healing Touch Program. (2014). *Level 3 notebook (6ᵗʰ ed.)*. San Antonio, TX: author

Healing Touch Program. (2013). *Level 4/5 notebook (4ᵗʰ ed.)*. San Antonio, TX: author

Hochachka, P.W., Monge, C. (2000). Evolution of human hypoxia tolerance physiology. *Advances in Experimental and Medical Biology, 475*, 25–43.

Hover-Kramer, D. (2011 a). *Creating healing relationships: professional standards for energy therapy practitioners*. Santa Rosa CA: Energy Psychology Press.

Hover-Kramer, D. (2013 b). *Healing touch guidebook: practicing the art and science of Human Caring*, San Antonio, TX, Healing Touch Program.

Hovland, S. (2012). *Anatomy for healers: level 1 notebook (Class Handout)*. Sue Hovland Healing Therapies, Littleton, CO.

Hunt, V. (1996). *Infinite mind: science of the human vibrations of consciousness*. Malibu, CA: Malibu Publishing.

Iyenar, B.K.S. (1995). *Light on yoga*. New York, NY: Schocken Books.

Iida, S., Matsumoto, S. (1978). *Vasubandhu's interpretaion of pratītya-samutpāda-ādi* [Class handout]. Department of Religious Studies, University of British Columbia, Vanouver, British Columbia, Canada

Jain, S., Pavlik, D., Distefan, J. Bruyere, R., Acer, J., Garcia, R.,…Mills, J. (2012). Complementary medicine for fatigue and cortisol variability in breast cancer survivors: a randomized controlled trial. *Cancer*, 118 (3), 777-787. doi: 10.1002/cncr.26345

Jain, S., McMahon, G. F., Hasen, P., Kozub, M. P., Porter, V., King, R., & Guarneri, E. M. (2012 b). Healing Touch with Guided Imagery for PTSD in returning active duty military: a randomized controlled trial. *Military medicine, 177*(9), 1015-1021.

Jonas, W.B. & Cruz, R.A. (2003). The role and importance of definitions and standards in healing research. *Alternative Therapies in Health and Medicine, 9* (3), A5-A9.

Jovanovic, P. (1995). *An inquiry into the existence of guardian angels.* New York, NY: M.Evans and Company.

Joy, W.B. (1979). *Joy's way: an introduction to the potentials for healing with body energies.* New York, NY: Penguin Putnam Inc.

Kkanakura, Y. (1980). *Hindu-buddhist thought in India.* Yokohama, Japan: Hokke Journal, Inc.

Kaminoff, L., Matthews, A. (2012). *Yoga anatomy 2nd ed.* Champaign, IL: Human Kinetics.

Laszlo, E. (2009). *The akashic experience: science and the cosmic memory field.* Rochester, NY: Inner Traditions.

Lawrenz, F. (1986). Misconceptions of physical science concepts among elementary school teachers. *School Science and Mathematics, 86* (8), 654-660.

Lavitt, J. (2016). Addiction is a response to childhood suffering: in depth with Gabor Maté. Retrieved from https://www.thefix.com/gabor-maté-addiction-holocaust-disease-trauma-recovery?page=all

Leopold, A. (1986). *A Sand County Almanac: with essays on conservation from Round River.* Ballintine Books

Liboff, A. (2008). *Toward an electromagnetic paradigm for biology and medicine.* Retrieved from http://www.liebertonline.com/doi/pdf/10.1089/107555304322848940.

Lipton, Bruce H. (2005). *The biology of belief.* Santa Rosa, CA: Mountain of Love Elite Books.

Lutgendorf, S., Mullen-Houser, E., Russell, D., DeGeest, K., Jacobson, G., Hart, L., ... & Lubaroff, D. M. (2010). Preservation of immune function in cervical cancer patients during chemoradiation using a novel integrative approach. *Brain, behavior, and immunity, 24*(8), 1231-1240.

Lund, E. (1947). *Bioelectric fields and growth*. Austin, TX: University of Texas.

MacIntyre, B., Hamilton, J., Fricke, T., Ma, W., Mehle, S., & Michel, M. (2008). The efficacy of healing touch in coronary artery bypass surgery recovery: a randomized clinical trial. *Alternative therapies in health and medicine, 14*(4), 24.

Maville, J. A., Bowen, J. E., & Benham, G. (2008). Effect of healing touch on stress perception and biological correlates. *Holistic nursing practice, 22*(2), 103-110

Mate, G. (2004). *When the body says no: the cost of hidden stress*. Toronto, ON: Vintage Canada.

McCraty, R., Atkinson, M. and Bradley, R. T. (2004). Electrophysiological Evidence of Intuition: Part 1. The Surprising Role of the Heart. *Journal of Alternative and Complementary Medicine*, 10(1), pp. 133-143.

McCraty, R., & Zayas, M. (2010). Cardiac coherence, self-regulation, autonomic stability, and psychosocial wellbeing. *Front. Psychol.* 5:1090. doi:10.3389/fpsyg.2014.01090

McMurray, W. C. (1977) *Essentials of human metabolism: the relationships of biochemistry to human physiology and disease*. San Francisco, CA: Harper and Row.

McTaggart, L. (2002 a). *The field: the quest for the secret forces of the universe*. New York, NY: Harper Collins.

McTaggart, L. (2007 b). *The intention experiment: Using your thoughts to change your life and the world*. New York, NY: Simon & Schuster.

Miller, L., Balodis, I., McClintock, C., Xu, J., Lacadie, C., Sinha, R., Potenza, M. (2018). Neural Correlates of Personalized Spiritual Experiences. *Cerebral Cortex*, bhy 102. doi:10.1093/cercor/bby102

Montgomery, C. (2013). *Happy city: transforming our lives through urban design*. Anchor Canada

Muehsam, D. (2018). *Emotional state of mind and health*. Retrieved from Consciousness and Healing Initiative information webstite https://www.chi.is/good-vibes-better-health-emerging-science-positive-emotional-state-mind-health/

Myss, C. (1996). *Anatomy of the spirit: the seven stages of power and healing.* New York, NY: Harmony Books.

National Institute for the Clinical Application of Behavioral Medicine. (2018). *Is there a factor that can predict PTSD development in war veterans?* Retrieved from https://www.nicabm.com/is-there-a-factor-that-can-predict-ptsd-development-in-war-veterans/

Noontil, A. (2002). *The body is the barometer of the soul.* Kilsyth South, Victoria, AU: Bruby Books.

Nummenmaa, L., Glerean, E., Hari, R., Hietanen, J. (2013). Bodily maps of emotions. *PNAS,* Early edition, 1-6. doi: 10.1073/pnas.1321664111

Nutrition Wonderland. (2009). *Understanding our bodies: Dopamine and its rewards.* Retrieved from http://nutritionwonderland.com/2009/07/understanding-our-bodies-dopamine-rewards/

Ogawa, T., & deBold, A. (2014). The heart as an endocrine organ. *Endocrine Connections,* 3(2), R31-R34. doi:10.1530/EC-14-0012

Ornish, D (1998). *Love and survival: 8 pathways to intimacy and health.* New York, NY: HarperCollins Publishers, Inc.

Oschmann, J. (2006). *Energy medicine: the scientific basis.* Toronto, ON: Churchill Livingstone.

Paigi, S., Klein, E., Shamay-Tsory, S. (2016). Oxytocin improves compassion toward women among patients with PTSD. *Psychoneuroendocrinology,* 64, 143-149. doi:10.1016/j.psyneuren.2015.11.008

Peirce, P. (2009). *Frequency: the power of personal vibration.* New York, NY: Atria Books, A Division of Simon and Schuster.

Pert, C. (1997). *Molecules of emotion.* New York, NY: Scribner.

Perry, A., Bentin, S., Shalev, I., Israel, S., Uzefovsky, F., Bar-On, D., Ebstein, R. (2010). Intranasal oxytocin moduclates EEG mu/alpha and beta rhythms during perception of biological motion. *Psychoneuroendocrinology,* 35 (10), 1449-1453. doi: 10.1016/j.psyneuen.2010.04.011

Petrucci, R. (1989). *General chemistry: principles and modern applications (5th ed).* New York, NY: Macmillan Publishing Company.

Pierrehumbert, S., Torrisi, R., Laufer, D., Halfon, O., Ansermet, F., Beck Popovic, M.(2010). Oxytocin response to an experimental psychosocial challenge in adults exposed to traumatic experiences during childhood or adolescence. *Neuroscience,* 166(1), 168-177. doi: 10.1016/j.neuroscience.2009.12.016

Porges, S. (2007). The polyvagal perspective. *Biol.Psychol, 74, 116-143.* doi:10.1016/j.biopsycho.2006.06.009

Post-White, J., Kinney, M. E., Savik, K., Gau, J. B., Wilcox, C., & Lerner, I. (2003). Therapeutic massage and healing touch improve symptoms in cancer. *Integrative Cancer Therapies, 2*(4), 332-344.

Post, S. (2005). Altruism, happiness, and health; it's good to be good. *International Journal of Behavioral Medicine, 12 (2), 66-77.*

Redwood, D. (2002). Methodological changes in the evaluation of complementary and alternative medicine: issues raised by Sherman et al. And Hawk et al. (2002). *The Journal of Alternative and Complementary Medicine, 8* (1), 5-6.

Rein, G. (2004). Bioinformation within the biofield: beyond bioelectromagnetics. *Journal of Alternative and Complementary Medicine,* 10(1): 59-68.

Richardson, J. (2002). Evidence-based complementary medicine: Rigor, relevance, and the swampy lowlands. *The Journal of Alternative and Complementary Medicine, 3,* 221-223.

Rolf, I., (1977). *Rolfing: reestablishing the natural alignment and structural integration of the human body for vitality and well-being.* Rochester, VT: Healing Arts Press.

Ropp, T. (2017). 12 Ways to unlock the powers of the vagus nerve. Retrieved from https://upliftconnect.com/12-ways-unlock-powers-vagus-nerve/

Rosenthal, M. (2017). Seven reasons your addiction makes perfect sense. Retrieved from http://upliftconnect.com/your-addiction-makes-perfect sense/?utm_source=UPLIFT&utm_campaign =f64660b983

Rubik, B., Muehsam, D., Hammerschlag, D., Shamini, J. (2015). Biofield science and healing: history, terminology, and concepts. *Global Advances in Health Medicine,* 2015; 4(suppl):8-14.doi: 10.7453/gahmj.2015.038.supp.

Ryff, C., Singer, H. (2006). Know thyself and become what you are: a eudaimonic approach to psychological wellbeing. *Journal of Happiness Studies,* 2006: 13-29

Schwartz, G., Simon, W. (2007). *The energy healing experiments.* New York, NY: Atria Books.

Seskevich, J. E., Crater, S. W., Lane, J. D., & Krucof, M. W. (2004). Beneficial effects of noetic therapies on mood before percutaneous intervention for unstable coronary syndromes. *Nursing research, 53*(2), 116-121.

Shaffer, F., McCraty, R., Zerr, C. (2014). A healthy heart is not a metronome: an integrative review of the heart's anatomy and heart rate variability. *Frontiers in Psychology,* 5, 1040. Retrieved online from https://www.ncbi.nlm.nih.gov/pmc/articles/PMC4179748/. doi: 10.3389/fpsyg.2014.01040

Sheldrake, R. (2009). *Morphic resonance: the nature of formative causation.* Rochester, VT: Park Street Press.

Smith, F. (2017). The addicted brain. *National Geographic, 252 (3), 30-55.*

Stryer, Lubert (1975). Biochemistry. W.H. Freeman & Co. San Francisco, CA.

Storoni, M., (2015). *The science behind yoga and stress.* Retrieved from Uplift website https://upliftconnect.com/yoga-and-stress/

Taber's Cyclopedic Medical Dictionary 21st ed., (2009) F.A. Davis Company, Philadelphia, PA.

Takahashi, T (1994). *Atlas of the human body.* New York, NY: Harper Collins Publishing Inc.

Talbot, M. (1992). *The holographic universe.* New York, NY: Harper Collins Publishers.

Tsai, S., Lin, Y., Chu, S., Hsu, C., Cheng, S., (2010). Interpretation and use of natriuretic peptides in non-congestive heart failure settings. *Yonsei Medical Journal,* 5 (2), 151-163. doi: 10.3349/ymj.2010.51.2.151

Van der Wall, E. E. and van Gilst, W. H. (2013). Neurocardiology: Close interaction between heart and brain. *Netherlands Heart Journal,* 21(2), pp. 51–52. http://doi.org/10.1007/s12471-012-0369-4

Walach, H. (2001). The efficacy paradox in randomized controlled trials of CAM and elsewhere: beware of the placebo trap. *The Journal of Alternative and Complementary Medicine, 7* (3), 213-218.

Wallentin, M., HojlundNielsen, A., Vuust, P., Dohn, A., Roepstprff, A., EllegaardLund, T. (2011). Amygdala and heart rate variability responses from listening to emotionally intense parts of a story. *Neuroimage,* 58(3), 963-973. doi: 10.1016/j.neuroimage.2011.06.077

Warber, S.L., Gordon, A., Gillispie, B.W., Olson, M., Assefi, N. (2003). Standards for conducting clinical biofield energy healing research. *Alternative Therapies in Health and Medicine, 9* (3), A54-64.

Whelton, S., Chin, A., Xin, X., He, J. (2002). Effect of aerobic exercise on blood pressure: a meta-analysis of randomized, controlled trials. *Ann Intern Med.* 2002; 136(7), 493-503. doi:10.7326/0003-4819-136-7-200204020-00006

World Health Organization. (2018). *The top 10 causes of death.* Retrieved from http://www.who.int/mediacentre/factsheets/fs310/en/index3.html/8

Zohar, A. H., Cloninger, C. R. and McCraty, R. (2013). Personality and Heart Rate Variability: Exploring Pathways from Personality to Cardiac Coherence and Health. *Open Journal of Social Sciences,* 1(06), pp. 32.

Zak, P.J., Stanton, A.A., Ahmadi, S. (2007). Oxytocin increases generosity in humans. *PLOS ONE,* 2007: ell28.

INDEX

EQ (emotional intelligence
quotient) 165
eudaimonia, 154

F

Faraday, Michael 53, 74
fentanyl 113
fermentation, 27
Feynman, Richard 79
field 23, 53, 54, 56, 71, 74, 97
forgiveness 142, 159, 160, 162,
164, 179
Frank, Anne 175
Franklin, Benjamin 53
Frankl, Viktor 170
frequency 74, 76, 77
functional magnetic resonance imaging
(fMRI) 177

G

GABA (gamma amino butyric
acid) 162
Galileo Galilei 47
Galvani, Luigi 51
Gamma 148
Gamma rays 75
Gibran, Kabril 179
glucose 20, 25, 27, 28, 137
glycine 116
glycolysis 26
gratitude 121, 142, 145, 146, 159, 161,
162, 164, 179
Grave's disease 21
Greek cities 154
Grey, Alex xix

H

happiness xvi, 111, 135, 137, 138, 154,
155, 156, 162, 179
Harvey, William xix
Hay, Louise 146
Healing Touch Program 43

heart coherence 125, 127, 161
heart rate variability (HRV) 125, 177
Heart Rate Variability (HRV) 68
Heisenberg, Werner 89
Helium 60
hemoglobin 10
hemorrhage 21
heroin. 113
Herschel, William 72
hertz 77, 78
Hertz. Heinrich 74
high blood pressure 21, 29, 40
Hochaka, Peter 182
Holden, Robert 156
hope 41, 157, 164, 167, 170, 171, 172,
173, 175, 179
Huygens, Christian 72
Hydrogen 60
hydromorphone 113
hypertension 21, 156
hypoglossal nerve 42

I

induction 84, 85
inert 60
inferior vena cava 9
inflammation 73, 112, 119, 138,
162, 174
Infra-Low 149
infrared (IR) 72
intercostals 35
interleukin-6 174
intuition 100, 139, 140, 147, 178, 179
ionic 62, 64
ionizing radiation 75
ionosphere 55
ions 52, 57, 62, 63, 64, 66
IQ (intelligence quotient) 165

J

James Oschmann 145
James, William 45

Printed in the United States
By Bookmasters